Just as I Am
Hymns Affirming the Divine Female

a Girl God Hermnal

Edited by Trista Hendren,
Sharon Smith
and Pat Daly

Cover Art by Kat Shaw

©2021 All Rights Reserved
ISBN: 978-82-93725-21-3

www.thegirlgod.com

Girl God Books

Re-membering with Goddess: Healing the Patriarchal Perpetuation of Trauma

Re-Membering with Goddess is an anthology of women's experiences of trauma—trauma as a result of patriarchy; trauma perpetuated by patriarchy; and how through personal healing of trauma the Goddess is re-membered, re-embodied and resurrected. As repeating loops of trauma restriction release—in the mind, body and nervous system—Goddess is re-embodied and rises... and the patriarchy falls.

Willendorf's Legacy: The Sacred Body

Travel through time and discover a world where the fullness of women was both admired and deified. Reclaim your beautiful Goddess body through the rich pages of this powerful collection of art, poetry and essays celebrating our divine inheritance as daughters of Willendorf.

New Love: a reprogramming toolbox for undoing the knots

A powerful combination of emotional/spiritual techniques, art and inspiring words for women who wish to move away from patriarchal thought. *New Love* includes a mixture of compelling thoughts and suggestions for each day, along with a "toolbox" to help you change the parts of your life you want to heal.

How to Live Well Despite Capitalist Patriarchy

A book challenging societal assumptions to help women become stronger and break free of their chains. Written by Trista Hendren.

The Girl God

A book for children young and old, celebrating the Divine Female by Trista Hendren. Magically illustrated by Elisabeth Slettnes with quotes from various faith traditions and feminist thinkers.

Tell Me Why
A feminist twist of the creation story told with love from a mother
to her son, in hopes of crafting a different world for them both.
Written by Trista Hendren / Illustrated by Elisabeth Slettnes.

Original Resistance: Reclaiming Lilith, Reclaiming Ourselves
This anthology—a chorus of voices hitting chords of defiance,
liberation, anger and joy—reclaims the goodness of women bold
enough to hold tight to their essence. Through poetry, prose,
incantation, prayer and imagery, women from all walks of life
invite you to join them in the revolutionary act of claiming their
place—of reclaiming themselves.

Re-visioning Medusa: from Monster to Divine Wisdom
A remarkable collection of essays, poems, and art by scholars who
have researched Her, artists who have envisioned Her, and women
who have known Her in their personal story. All have spoken with
Her and share something of their communion in this anthology.

Inanna's Ascent: Reclaiming Female Power
Inanna's Ascent examines how females can rise from the
underworld and reclaim their power, sovereignly expressed
through poetry, prose and visual art. All contributors are
extraordinary women in their own right, who have been through
some difficult life lessons—and are brave enough to share their
stories.

On the Wings of Isis: Reclaiming the Sovereignty of Auset
For centuries, women have lived, fought and died for their
equality, independence and sovereignty. Originally known as
Auset, the Egyptian Goddess Isis reveals such a path. Unfurl your
wings and join an array of strong women who have embodied
the Goddess of Ten Thousand Names to celebrate their authentic
selves.

Complete list of Girl God publications at www.thegirlgod.com

Dedicated to every girl-child who grew up singing songs that did not affirm her Divinity.

In honor and appreciation of the tremendous life's work of Carol P. Christ.

(1945-2021)

Table of Contents

"Sing it!
Nothing
that can be remembered
with love,
can ever be lost!"

-Dr. Clarissa Pinkola Estes

So... What's a HERmnal?

Sharon Smith

"A *what?* What's a 'hermnal?'" That's a question I've been asked repeatedly whenever I've mentioned this collection of rewritten hymns from Girl God Books. And it's a question that's both easy and somewhat difficult to answer. The easy part: It's a book of praise songs to the Great Mother Goddess. The "somewhat difficult" part: Explaining, to those comfortable with Patriarchy, why we need one in the first place.

We've been inundated with images and stories and pronouns that define the Creator as "masculine-only": The Almighty One; the "King of kings and Lord of lords," the Eternal Father"—always referenced with the masculine pronouns "He," "Him," "His;" never with the feminine pronouns "She," "Her" or "Hers." This has become so deeply ingrained into all aspects of our culture that many cannot envision the Divine as anything but "masculine-only." To think of God as female is silly at best...and blasphemous at its worst.

But something has been happening over the past several decades: Women are awakening. We're remembering who we are. And we're done with patriarchal stories that cast us in a "lesser-than" role; that punish us for "Eve's disobedience" in the Garden of Eden which, according to the Patriarchs, resulted in the damnation of Mankind—and all the pain and suffering that has resulted from her "rebellion." So we're leaving traditional patriarchal churches to find something that better aligns with our Feminine Intuition and Deep Ancestral Knowing. And we're rediscovering the Goddess: The Divine Feminine. The "Great SHE." The Creatrix. The Mother of All.

When Trista came to me with the idea of creating a book of rewritten hymns in praise of the Great Mother, I was beyond excited. "This is something we *really* need," I told her. To my knowledge, there hasn't been a complete book of worship songs to the Goddess. So we began brainstorming. Trista came up with the title, "Just As I Am: Hymns Affirming the Divine Female" and we settled on the beautiful, body-positive artwork of Kat Shaw for the cover. Then we subtitled the work, "A Girl God Hermnal."

With emphasis on the HER.

And why not? The Goddess has been in the background for five millennia, while the patriarchal "Father God" has monopolized the stage—and the spotlight. Now it's HER turn to shine! And shine She does through the beautiful, inspiring Herms and artwork of so many talented, Goddess-loving Women included in this book.

What is a Hermnal? It's the collective sigh of our ancestral Grandmothers. It's a means of drawing us closer together as Sisters. It is a compilation of songs that affirms our Sacredness, apart from Man, and assures us that we are Sovereign Beings and Creatrixes, too. And it is our Love Gift of Gratitude to Mama.

We hope you will enjoy these Herms and use them often in your Circles, Services, and Ceremonies.

May Goddess be praised... and may She bless you all!

A Note on Styles, Preferences and Language
Trista Hendren

Just as I am contains a variety of writing styles from women around the world. Various forms of English are included in this anthology and we chose to keep spellings of the writers' place of origin to honor/honour each unique voice.

It was the expressed intent of the editors to not police standards of citation, transliteration and formatting. Contributors have determined which citation style, italicization policy and transliteration system to adopt in their pieces. The result reflects the diversity of academic fields, genres and personal expressions represented by the authors.[1]

Mary Daly wrote long ago that, "Women have had the power of naming stolen from us."[2] The quest for our own naming, and our own language, is never-ending, and each of us attempts it differently.

People often get caught up on whether we say *Goddess* or *Girl God*—or *Divine Female* vs. *Divine Feminine*. Personally, I try to just listen to what the speaker is trying to say. The fact remains that few of us were privileged with a woman-affirming education—and we all have a lot of time to make up for. Let's all be gentle with each other through that process.

If you find that a particular re-write doesn't sit well with you, please feel free to use the Al-Anon suggestion: "Take what you

---

1   This paragraph is borrowed and adapted with love from *A Jihad for Justice: Honoring the Work and Life of Amina Wadud*. Edited by Kecia Ali, Juliane Hammer and Laury Silvers.

2   Daly, Mary. *Gyn/Ecology: The Metaethics of Radical Feminism*. Beacon Press, 1990.

like, leave the rest!" You can also adjust the lyrics and make them your own.

Re-writing and singing these Hermns has been deeply healing for me. I wish the same blessing for each reader as you sing along to the new versions of these hymns.

I had hoped to also publish our Solstice Carol Book this year, but my schedule would not allow it. While I intend to dedicate that book to the memory of Carol P. Christ, it seems impossible not to mention her inspiration on this project. I write this in tears, still in grief over losing her too soon. She was an enormously powerful woman—both physically and intellectually—and, in my mind at least, incapable of dying anytime soon.

Carol lived large and stood tall. She was the embodiment of a strong woman and one of the brightest women I have ever met. Her work was tremendously important to me as someone whose life was wounded by Christianity. I will be forever grateful.

As Carol noted in *Laughter of Aphrodite*, "When singing to the Father and Son, a girl must hear her exclusion. She must begin to recognize that the power and the glory are not to be hers."[3]

I certainly felt that rejection growing up.

While I have read many affirming words over the years, there is something entirely different about singing these words. Singing is an embodied experience. The vibrations reach the deepest wounded parts of the psyche.

Singing with other sisters on Pilgrimage in Crete gave me my first glimpse of what intoning woman-affirming songs could do for my soul. I am so grateful that I was able to bring my (then) 12-year-

---

3   Christ, Carol P. *Laughter of Aphrodite: Reflections on a Journey to the Goddess*. HarperCollins; Reprint edition, 1988.

old daughter to experience that with me much earlier in life. It has always been my hope that Helani will not have to spend so many decades reprogramming herself. The work of Carol P. Christ—and others—paved new neural pathways for women of all generations. I am honored to share a few of Carol's hymns here.

I know she will be singing these right along with us.

May she rest in power and in peace.

The Wounding
Trista Hendren

I grew up singing in the church, as often as they'd let me. I was in choir and frequently did solos—or duets with my sister. When I went off to college, I signed up for everything available to me, traveling to various churches—and even rather frightening male prisons—to sing songs about Jesus.

When I lost my faith during my first year at school, I stopped singing.

I always sang as a sort of solace, finding comfort in my faith that God would protect me and provide. I had no reference point anymore. It was too painful.

About 7 years later, my father asked me to sing at his wedding. It should have been a fairly easy song for me—*Feels Like Home* by Linda Ronstadt—but I had lost the power in my vocal cords. My dad was shocked at the rehearsal, and chastised me in front of his friend, who was accompanying me. "What happened to your voice?" he jeered.

It took me nearly 2 decades to find it again.

I don't know how I got through singing at his wedding. I was still his faithful daughter at that time, so backing out was not an option. I knew he would be disappointed with my performance no matter what I did at that point: There was no time to build my voice back up the week before his wedding.

I vowed to never sing in public again.

It took many years of love and encouragement from my husband to get me singing again. But I have never felt the confidence I was once able to muster in front of other people.

One of our pastimes is to sing together at night. If we have a few close friends over, I will sing with them, too. We have been re-writing hymns and Christmas Carols for many years. My voice has slowly gotten stronger, but I am not certain it will ever come back to where it once was. Frankly, I don't have the time in my schedule to devote to it at this point in my life. My perfectionist tendencies have weakened with age though—and, being surrounded by love, instead of criticism, has also been deeply healing.

Intellectually, I know that in order to thrive, Goddess songs and chants are nurturing to my soul in a way that no other music can be. Yet, I still often turn the goofy Norwegian Country music channel on while cooking dinner instead. While I admit I am still sometimes homesick, there is more to it. The songs we grow up singing provide a false sense of comfort. It takes time to ease into new songs.

It takes practice to learn new words when the old ones are seared into our brains. Even the songs I have re-written myself still do not come out easily. I have to read the words—they have not replaced the old ones in my soul yet. Silence, submission and fear still remain with me—even all these years later.

Sue Monk Kidd wrote, "And what does a girl, who is forming her identity, do with all the scriptures admonishing women to submission and silence? Having them 'explained away' as a product of an ancient time does not entirely erase her unease. She also experiences herself missing from pronouns in scripture, hymns and prayers. And most of all, as long as God "himself" is exclusively male, she will experience the otherness, the lessness, of herself; all the pious talk in the world about females being equal to males will fail to compute in the deeper places inside her."[4] These toxic scriptures have taken my entire lifetime to even begin to overcome.

This Hermnal is a tool to help you break free of the indoctrination of inferiority most of us were raised with. In doing so, we hope to rattle the cage that women have been locked up in for thousands of years.

To do so, we need each other. As Mary Daly wrote:

> "Clearly, there is no simple 'one-shot' cure for a lifetime of conditioning to dependence. Women can raise each other's consciousness of it, and encourage each other to take the risks necessary to become free."[5]

Our first Zoom Sing-Along with Shellee Layne was a riling consciousness-raising for many of us. Some words were triggering —and discussing that in community was healing in-and-of itself.

Our socialization as girls was deep and thorough. Many of us spent hours a day pouring over disabling scriptures. Nawal El Saadawi stated that, "You cannot exploit people without controlling their brains."[6] There are people who have memorized the entire Quran. I never went nearly that far, but growing up as a Christian I could recite hundreds of verses, many of which I can still remember without having picked up a Bible for a very long time.

The hymns I grew up singing had an even deeper effect on me. I can still sing all of them from heart. When my grandparents were

---

4   Kidd, Sue Monk. *The Dance of the Dissident Daughter: A Woman's Journey from Christian Tradition to the Sacred Feminine.* HarperOne; 1996.

5   Daly, Mary. *Beyond God the Father: Toward a Philosophy of Women's Liberation.* Beacon Press; Revised Edition, 1993.

6   El Saadawi, Nawal. "Women, Creativity and Dissidence." *The Essential Nawal El Saadawi.* Zed Books; 2010. First published in 2006 as The Seventh International AWSA Conference.

dying, I came back to them often, singing at the top of my lungs in my car on my way to care for them and back. They were comforting—but not *affirming*.

Patricia Lynn Reilly wrote, "It was a deeply belittling experience to sit in services week after week that excluded us from the language and imagery used in the liturgy, hymns, and sermons; and that marginalized or ignored the contributions, concerns, and realities of a woman's life."[7]

It must be said that Sharon Smith and I went through these revised hymns again and again and again to make sure we had weeded out any sense of shame, blame or judgment. And, that was *after* each hymn had already been carefully re-written. There is still a lot of deconstructing to do.

These songs are so ingrained in most of us that it takes many years of undoing to even understand that they are problematic.

We must be diligent about absorbing new texts and songs that empower us as women. And, I don't think Gender-neutral language goes far enough. There is too much baggage in Father-God language. As Carol P. Christ wrote:

> "Even people who no longer 'believe in God' or participate in the institutional structure of patriarchal religion still may not be free of the power of the symbolism of God the Father. A symbol's effect does not depend on rational assent, for a symbol also functions on levels of the psyche other than the rational. Symbol systems cannot simply be rejected; they must be replaced. Where there is no replacement, the mind will revert to familiar structures at times of crisis, bafflement, or defeat."[8]

---

7   Reilly, Patricia Lynn. *Be Full of Yourself!: The Journey from Self-Criticism to Self-Celebration.* Open Window Creations; 1998.
8   Christ, Carol P. "Why Women Need the Goddess." Presented as the keynote address to an audience of over 500 at the "Great Goddess Re-emerging"

I believe that re-writing the songs we grew up with is critically important if we are to rise from our subordinate status as women. As Glenys Livingstone wrote, "It is not female biology that has betrayed the female... it is the stories and myths we have come to believe about ourselves."[9]

It is time to tell different stories. It is time to sing and chant them too.

I remember sitting inside a cave in Crete on Pilgrimage with Carol P. Christ where she read, "We Need a God Who Bleeds Now" by Ntozake Shange. I knew the poem well, but hearing Carol read it so forcefully shook something deep inside me.

While I have had the privilege of having several wonderful female pastors, they were never particularly affirming of my womanhood or my divinity. They *certainly* never affirmed my period. Carol read the poem with such conviction and clarity that no other world seemed possible. It was both a realization and a deep healing all at once when she boldly proclaimed:

> "i am
> not wounded i am bleeding to life"[10]

May we all find such a healing through the singing of these altered songs—and the reclamation of our stories and our power.

---

conference at the University of Santa Cruz in the spring of 1978. It was first published in Heresies: The Great Goddess Issue (1978), 8-13, and reprinted in Carol P. Christ and Judith Plaskow, eds., Womanspirit Rising: A Feminist Reader on Religion (San Francisco: Harper & Row, 1979), 273-287, as well as in Carol P. Christ, Laughter of Aphrodite: Reflections on a Journey to the Goddess (San Francisco: Harper & Row, 1987) 117-132. I 1978.

9 Livingstone, Glenys. *PaGaian Cosmology: Re-inventing Earth-based Goddess Religion.* iUniverse, Inc.; 2005. p 77.

10 Shange, Ntozake. *For Colored Girls Who Have Considered Suicide When the Rainbow Is Enuf.* Scribner; 1997.

Putting Her Voice Back
Ama Baartz

Singing Is a Sacred Power

Carolyn Lee Boyd

A moss-soft ballad sung from a mountain top to the sunrise. A parent's lullaby to soothe a newborn to sleep. Thousands of voices rising together to banish injustice from our planet. A single wavering melody infusing inspiration into a moment of despair. Whenever we open our mouths to sing, no matter how tuneful or discordant our song, we have instant access to a well of power to transform ourselves and others.

Over the years, I've been amazed at how often singing denotes spiritual power in myths and stories about goddesses and holy women from across the globe and throughout time. These are just a few examples from around the world. You may know others.

The first woman, Asintmah, of the Athabascan people of Canada, wove a blanket of fireweed blossoms which she spread over the Earth as she began to sing, causing the Earth to give birth to all the animals on our planet.

The young Chinese heroines Gum Lin and Loy Yi Lung sang to mesmerize a dragon so they could unlock a gate that let waters flow down a mountain to save their village.

The Norse prophetesses called Volva told of the future by chanting.

Japan's Yuki-Onne eased the passing of those trapped in blizzards by singing them to sleep, then breathing cold on them until they died peacefully and painlessly.

Some singing by goddesses and holy women is more malevolent. The Celtic Morrigan sang charms before battles to ensure victory for her side — good for her people, but not so good for her foes.

The Sirens enchanted Greek sailors by singing, luring them to their deaths.

Of course, 21st century life is full of singing and chanting as part of religious liturgy or personal spiritual practice as well as inspiring positive societal change. I also find that many people find the greatest solace in songs that come from their religious tradition, especially if learned in childhood. I think this speaks to the ability of music to express spiritual and socially inspirational ideas and connect us in ways that spoken words alone cannot. I find I often sing as part of my own spiritual practice, for example, often serenading the land, or a plant or wild animal as a form of offering.

Perhaps one reason for these stories of magical singing is the physical and emotional benefits recently confirmed by medical research. Singing causes the release of endorphins and oxytocin, which lifts mood, and is related to lower levels of the stress hormone cortisol. Older people who sing in choirs are less lonely and more engaged in life. Studies of music in general show a slew of benefits to physical, mental, and emotional functioning.

Besides affirming that the power of singing was as robust in our past as in our present, the myths and stories teach us about the power of singing beyond its physiological and emotional effects. In our culture, in which women's spiritual power has been demonized and devalued, it can sometimes feel difficult to grasp exactly what our inner power is and how to use it. We may even find ourselves fearing it, unconsciously or consciously. Singing by ourselves or with others and really allowing ourselves to experience its transformative force, affirms to us that our spiritual power is real, and that it is beautiful and awe-inspiring. We can know that our spiritual power is to be embraced for making the world the paradise it is meant to be.

Singing reminds us that our spiritual power is already within us as a part of our most essential being, both physical and spiritual. It is not outside of us or needing to be conferred by another entity, divine or human, but as much an element of our lives and ourselves as breathing in and out.

Singing reminds us that our bodies are divine and holy, that we have the power to create immense beauty through our flesh and blood. Through singing we create vibrations that are not only heard but felt in the depths of our and others' being and connect us to the very cosmos.

Singing brings magic into the everyday world. We do not have to wait till we are in some ethereal place to hear the voices of angels — all we have to do is listen to our own singing and that of others who share our world with us. Singing is not an exalted, once in a lifetime miracle, but a joy to be shared whenever we like.

Sappho once wrote "Although they are only breath, words which I command are immortal." Sappho's poems were written to be sung. Like Sappho, our singing is both an everyday and an immortal act, an expression of our sacred power that is within us and accessible to us always. When we recognize this power and use it for the benefit of ourselves, other beings, and the Earth, we can perhaps, like those ancient goddesses and holy women, help to sing new and better realities into being.

First published in *Feminism and Religion* on May 23, 2021.

Resources:

Patricia Monaghan, *New Book of Goddesses and Heroines, Llewellyn Publications*, St. Paul, Minnesota, 2000.

Patricia Monaghan, *Encyclopedia of Goddesses and Heroines,* New World Library, Novato, California, 2014.

Merlin Stone, *Ancient Mirrors of Womanhood,* Beacon Press, Boston, Massachusetts, 1979.

Sappho, translated by Mary Barnard, University of California Press, Berkeley, California, 1958.

"We sing the hymn, *Morning Has Broken* which speaks of the Garden of Eden 'fresh from God's Word,' and of God's literal footstep on the first grass. We may think of it as a nice poetic metaphor, though the writer of the lyric obviously thought of it as the truth. But the story of Eden is not a nice poetic metaphor, nor is it true. It is a lie born out of ignorance, and what's more, it is a pernicious lie that has caused an unimaginably huge amount of unnecessary human suffering over the centuries. It is the source of the doctrines of original sin, female inferiority and the damnation of disbelievers. The evils rooted in this myth still continue. There are still millions of people willing to kill or to die for Old Testament lies. There are millions of people who despise scientific enlightenment, who forbid real education for their children, who hate their neighbors if they disagree with Bible mythology. Battles are still fought, and will go on being fought, over religious nonsense. This is one of the greatest human follies: Perhaps this is even what might be called the real original sin."
-Barbara G. Walker, *Man Made God*

*Eve Cast Out**

Susan Klahr

*The original title of this painting is unknown. It is paired with Donna J. Snyder's poem of the same name, which was dedicated to Susan Klahr's memory in the *Jesus, Muhammad and The Goddess anthology.* The painting is shared with the permission of Ms. Klahr's family.

Freshness of Morning
(Sung to *Morning Has Broken*)
Dr Lynne Sedgmore

Freshness of morning brings every new day
Beauty of birdsong sweetens the air
Hear the bird chorus, feel new beginnings
Nature's abundance filling the world

Taste the moist rainfall, gifted from Gaia
Walk on the wetness, barefoot delight
Ours is the beauty of innocent mornings
Sunlight reflecting, shining so bright

Ours are the blessings of each new morning
Lifting our spirits, love everywhere
We are the oneness, always rebirthing
Precious new moments, together to share

Freshness of morning brings every new day
Beauty of birdsong sweetens the air
Hear the bird chorus, feel new beginnings
Nature's abundance filling the world

Darkness is Swirling
(Sung to *Morning has Broken*)

Kay Louise Aldred

Darkness is swirling
Like the first cauldron,
Stars bright are glowing
Like the first Light.
Praise for the silence!
Praise for the night-time!
Praise for the birthing
Fresh from the Womb!

Sweet the Breath's Lifeforce,
Light beams of Cosmos,
Like the first compounds -
Origin of Life.
Praise for the magic
Of earth, air, fire, water
Life in completeness
Where they unite.

Ours is darkness,
Ours is the night-time,
Born of pure chaos
Messy, disarray,
Praise with untamedness,
Praise every moon-time,
Goddess creating
Through death and decay.

Darkness is swirling
Like the first cauldron,
Starbright is twinkling
Like the first Light.
Praise for the silence!
Praise for the night-time!
Praise from them, birthing
Fresh from the Womb!

Goddess of the Cauldron
Kat Shaw

At the Cauldron
(Sung to *At the Cross*)
Sharon Smith

Verse 1

Alas! and did our Mothers bleed
And did our Mothers die?
They bowed their lovely sacred heads
For such as you and I!

Chorus:

At the Cauldron black as night,
Where I first saw the light
From the Womb of the Life-giving Flow;
There the Sacred Mystery of our Womanity
Is waiting for all people who would know.

Verse 2

They said 'twas sins our Mothers did,
That hanged them from a tree
And burned them at a wooden stake,
So we'd have sovereignty.

Chorus:

At the Cauldron black as night,
Where I first saw the light
From the Womb of the Life-giving Flow;
There the Sacred Mystery of our Womanity
Is waiting for all people who would know.

Verse 3
'Twas Patriarchy's brutal chains
That held our Mother's fast;
Yet they resisted through the pain,
So we'd be free at last!

Chorus:

At the Cauldron black as night
Where I first saw the light
From the womb of the Life-giving Flow
There the Sacred Mystery of our Womanity
Is waiting for all people who would know.

Our Mother
(Sung to *Our Father*)
Patricia Lynn Reilly

Our Mother, who art within us,
We celebrate your many names.
Your wisdom come. Your will be done,
Unfolding from the depths within us.

Each day you give us all that we need.
You remind us of our limits and we let go.
You support us in our power and we act with courage.

For you are the dwelling place within us,
the empowerment around us, and the celebration among us.
As it was in the very beginning, may it be now.

Originally published in *Words Made Flesh*.

She Who Is Our Mother! Goddess All-Lovely

(Sung to *Holy, Holy, Holy! Lord God Almighty*)

Sharon Smith

1. She who is our Mother; Goddess all-lovely!
Early in the morning we sing our songs to Thee.
She who is our Mother! We'll let it be known,
You're Goddess in Three Persons: Maiden, Mother, Crone!

2. She who is our Mother; your Daughters adore thee!
Dancing 'neath a golden Moon in sacred revelry;
Priestesses are gathered, placing flowers before thee,
Who was and is and evermore shall be!

3. She who is our Mother; Darkness cannot hide thee!
Though patriarchal men Your beauty could not see;
Only thou art Mother, creation doth decree.
You dwell here among us in Nature's majesty.

4. She who is our Mother; Goddess all-lovely!
Early in the morning we sing our songs to Thee.
She who is our Mother! We'll let it be known,
You're Goddess in Three Persons: Maiden, Mother, Crone!

Just as I Am

Trista Hendren

Just as I Am, without a plea,
For I know my blood is H-O-L-Y,
And what's been stolen can be found,
O Goddess Willendorf now, I am!

Just as I Am, so perfectly round
Just like my mother's supple mound;
And every inch of me is lovely,
O rounded Goddess, She is me!

Just as I Am, scorned and mocked
for I never fit into that box,
Now love and tenderness I embrace
O Goddess Willendorf, Here I am!

Just as I Am, softer each year;
I hug myself to hold Her dear;
For all this lushness I despised,
O rounded Goddess, You feel good!

Just as I Am, Thou wilt receive,
Wilt welcome, pardon, love, reprieve;
Because Thy beauty I now see,
O Goddess Willendorf, Blessed Be!

Author's note: This is my re-write of the classic hymn, written by Charlotte Elliott in 1835. *As someone who grew up with these hymns, and still have many of them embedded in my heart, I have wanted for years to re-write them in a woman-affirming way. Singing these new words has been healing for me.*

Goddess of Willendorf
Arna Baartz

There's Power in the Blood

Patricia Lynn Reilly

Imagine the sacraments and rituals of childhood commemorating the monthly shedding of a woman's blood, her sacred blood that holds within it both life and death.

Imagine singing songs and spirituals that celebrate the beautiful, powerful blood of woman. Imagine if you had sung these words in the synagogue, church, or home of your childhood.

Verse 1:
Would you be free from the burden of lies?
There's power in the blood, power in the blood.
Would you receive deep healing within?
There's wonderful power in the blood.

Chorus:
There is power, power, wonder-working power
in the blood of the woman.
There is power, power, wonder-working power
in the precious blood of the woman.

Verse 2:
Would you be wiser much wiser than now?
There's power in the blood, power in the blood.
Shame's stains are lost in her life-giving flow.
There's wonderful power in the blood.

Chorus:
There is power, power, wonder-working power
in the blood of the woman.
There is power, power, wonder-working power
in the precious blood of the woman.

Are You Washed in the Blood?

Trista Hendren

Have you been to Goddess to know old ways?
Are you washed in the blood of Goddess?
Do you fully feel Her ancient rituals now?
Are you washed in the blood of Goddess?

Are you washed in the blood,
In the shame cleansing blood of Goddess?
Are your garments scarlet
with Her menstrual flow?
Are you washed in the blood of Goddess?

Lay aside the dogma that is stained with shame,
And be washed in the blood of Goddess;
There's a fountain flowing that we all can claim,
To be washed in the blood of Goddess!

Are you washed in the blood,
In the shame cleansing blood of Goddess?
Are your garments scarlet
with Her menstrual flow?
Are you washed in the blood of Goddess?

She of the Dance
(Sung to *Simple Gifts*)
Rebekah Myers

I danced in the morning when the world was begun
I danced in the Moon and the Stars and the Sun
I created the Heavens, I created the Earth
I am She who gave them birth

Chorus:
Dance, dance around my holy Tree
I am the Queen of the Dance, said She
And I'll lead you all, whomever you may be
And I'll bless you all in the dance said She!

(Chorus)

I danced for my people, both the he and the she
Yet as time went on, he wouldn't honor me
And he cut me out of the story of our life
And he caused much pain and he caused much strife

(Chorus)

I still kept dancing, for the dance must go on
And my daughters remembered and they danced along
They rose from the shackles and they cast off the chains
And they taught all their brothers to dance again

(Chorus)

'Though he put you down, I will raise you high
For I am the Life that will never, ever die
I'll live in you, if you will live in Me
I am the Queen of the Dance, said She!

(Chorus)

Come Fly With Me
Cheryl Braganza

What Wondrous Love is This?

Alissa DeLaFuente

What wondrous love is this, O my soul, O my soul?
What wondrous love is this, O my soul?
What wondrous love is this that brought our great Goddess
To flood the Earth with gifts for my soul, body and soul,
To flood the Earth with gifts for my soul?

When I was sinking down, sinking down, sinking down,
When I was sinking down, sinking down,
When I was sinking down b'neath the wind and rain that hounds
Sister pine laid aside her crown for my soul, for my soul,
She laid aside her crown for my soul.

To the Goddess in the Trees I will sing, I will sing
To the Goddess in the Trees I will sing,
To the Goddess in the Trees who is the great I Am,
Alpha and Omega, I will sing, I will sing.
Alpha and Omega, I will sing.

And when from death I'm free, I'll sing on, I'll sing on,
And when from death I'm free, I'll sing on.
Through the Goddess in the Trees and the one in you and me,
I'll sing on, I'll sing on.
Through the Goddess in the Trees, I'll sing on.

In the lives of birds and bees, I'll sing on, I'll sing on.
And in the maple tree, may I sweeten life for thee;
Through eternity, I'll sing on.

What an Allyship in Goddess!
(Sung to *What a Friend We Have in Jesus*)
Kay Louise Aldred

What an Allyship in Goddess!
Admission through my holy blood,
What a joy to be born woman
Uniting for the highest good.
Oh, what pleasure I can access!
The entrance through my sacred bud,
By way of waves of ecstasy and rapture
I manifest my hallowed prayers.

Rooting deeply into Gaia
Knowing she holds all I need,
Breathing in her regulation
Her cycles, they become my lead.
In actualising as Sophia
I enthrone as Seer of the All,
The secrets of creative visioning
Is medicine I offer all.

We are powerful co-creators!
A gift that sometimes we forget,
Let Goddess fully be remembered,
And all desires be fully met.
Goddess IS our mind and body,
Evoke that truth immediately!
Embody all her blessed stories!
Future generations then are FREE!

Beautiful Mother

(Sung to *Fairest Lord Jesus*)
Ruth Calder-Murphy

Beautiful Mother,
Birther and Creator,
Spirit, who stirs every living thing,
You I will honour, Founder, Sustainer -
You make my soul rise up and sing.

Beauteous the meadows
and the verdant woodlands,
robed in the vestments of turning years,
You're in the flowers, soil, streams and birdsong,
there, your embrace relieves my fears.

Glorious the sunshine and the silver moonlight,
spiraling stars sing your boundless praise,
You are the splendour of all the galaxies,
nurturing darkness is your face.

Beautiful Mother,
Birther and Creator,
Daughter and Sister, Comfort, Friend,
glory and honour, praise, adoration
be yours forever, without end.

A Mighty Fortress

Ruth Calder-Murphy

A safe embrace is in Her arms,
our Mother, our Defender;
when pain and hardship circle round,
She is our soul's safe harbour.
When things around us rise to hasten our demise -
anxiety and grief -
She brings us sweet relief;
and peace is in her loving eyes.

In force and violence, suffering reigns
while hatred grows and festers
but in Her words is hope - and peace
flows in Her milk of kindness.
Her Spirit's all around,
where mothering love is found,
and through us flows the tide
connecting humankind
to Her transcendent tenderness.

The world is wide and beautiful
and Mother Nature's bounty
provides enough for all to live
in harmony and plenty.
When wars and hate and fear
make selfishness appear,
it pushes her away
and all her generous sway
is lost to greed and apathy.

Her words are sung upon the storm,
and whispered on the summer breeze,
She dances on the ocean wave
and paints Her heart in autumn leaves -
and though they try to frame
Her soul, Her voice, Her name
in terms that make Her less
or evil, or repressed,
eternal, true, She will remain.

Singing and Dancing to Your Own Tune
Barbara O' Meara

Weave Us Together, Queen
(Sung to *Bind us Together, Lord*)
Kay Louise Aldred

Weave us together Queen,
Weave us together
One heart that cannot be broken.
Weave us together Queen,
Weave us together
Weave us together as Love

There is always our wisdom,
There is always our truth.
There is always our body,
Within it the power of you.

Weave us together Queen,
Weave us together
One heart that cannot be broken.
Weave us together Queen,
Weave us together
Weave us together as Love.

Another Feminine rising,
The circle casting is done,
Birthed through the power of Goddess,
Humanity's change has begun.

Weave us together Queen,
Weave us together
One heart that cannot be broken.
Weave us together Queen,
Weave us together
Weave us together as Love.

How Great the Mother's Love for Us
(Sung to How Deep the Father's Love for Us)

Kate Hilderbrandt

How great the Mother's love for us
Shown vast throughout all nature
In summer, fall, winter and spring
In any kind of weather
Her sun and moon, they light our way
All paths for our exploring
With seed and fruit She blesses us
Abundance ever pouring

Behold the Mother and her young
Their lives upon her shoulders
She would not hold back anything
They have all their needs and pleasures
In animals, humans, and plants
She shows us how to mother
Both learning to care for ourselves
And to care for one another

I'll always boast in all Her gifts
Her flowers, mountains, waterfalls
Her beauty, soft and fierce at once
Draws awe and praise from one and all
Why should She lavish us this way?
With each and every season
Her nourishment, protection, love
Expands beyond all reason

She Lives
(Sung to *He Lives*)
Trista Hendren

I love a risen Goddess, She's in the world today
I know that She is living, whatever men may say
I see Her hand of mercy, I hear Her voice of cheer
And just the time I need Her She's always near

She lives (She lives), She lives (She lives),
The Goddess lives today
She walks with me and talks with me
Along life's marvelous way
She lives (She lives), She lives (She lives),
Reclaiming She imparts
You ask me how I know She lives?
She lives within my heart

In all the world around me I see Her loving care
And though my heart grows weary I never will despair
I know that She is leading, through all the stormy blast
The day of Her appearing will come at last

She lives (She lives), She lives (She lives),
The Goddess lives today
She walks with me and talks with me
Along life's narrow way
She lives (She lives), She lives (She lives),
Reclaiming She imparts
You ask me how I know She lives?
She lives within my heart

Rejoice, rejoice, O Women Lift up your voice and sing
Eternal hallelujahs[11] to Athena, our Queen
The Hope of all who seek Her, the Help of all who find
None other is so loving, so vast and kind

She lives (She lives), She lives (She lives),
The Goddess lives today
She walks with me and talks with me
Along life's narrow way
She lives (She lives), She lives (She lives),
Reclaiming She imparts
You ask me how I know She lives?
She lives within my heart

---

11 Laura Shannon noted during our *Medusa Speaks* series that the origins of
   "Hallelujah" are pre-patriarchal, announcing the birth of the Goddess.
   Shannon, Laura. *Medusa Speaks.* A Girl God Books online series re-storying
   Medusa. She is finishing a paper for the Solstice Carols Book that will dive
   deeper into this.

Amazing Grace (the Call of the Goddess)

Alissa DeLaFuente

Amazing grace
How sweet the sound
That saved someone like me.
I once was lost, but now I'm found,
Was blind, but now I see.

'Twas grace that taught my heart to feel,
And grace my fears relieved.
All hurt does lovingkindness heal
When we are truly seen.

Together in our earthly days,
May we sisters sing strong;
Let us embody all Her grace
And raise our voice in song!

My Goddess walks alongside me;
Her shield and sword bring might.
She comforts, cares, and mends despair.
She is both dark and light.

And when this mortal life shall fail,
And flesh and sense shall cease,
I shall be One with all of Love,
Of Life and Death, at peace.

Since She's been here millennia,
Bright shining like the sun,
We sing Her praise for all our days,
Until we are undone.

Shesus

Lisbeth Cheever-Gessaman

Turn Your Eyes Upon Goddess
(Sung to *Turn Your Eyes Upon Jesus*)
Sharon Smith

O Sister, are you deeply troubled,
No light in the darkness you see;
There's light if you look at the Goddess
And life more abundant and free.

Turn your eyes upon Goddess
Look full in Her wonderful face
And the natural goodness of Earth will shine
In the light of Her Love and Her Grace.

Her Wisdom shall guide you, Dear Sister;
Believe Her and all will be well;
Then go to the forest and find Her
She's waiting, Her stories to tell.

Turn your eyes upon Goddess,
Look full in Her wonderful face
And the natural goodness of Earth will shine
In the light of Her Love and Her Grace.

O Sister, please do not be troubled
Our Mother will always be near;
To strengthen and comfort Her Daughters,
So there is no reason to fear.

Turn your eyes upon Goddess
Look full in Her wonderful face
And the natural goodness of Earth will shine
In the light of Her Love and Her Grace.

The Heart of Love My Goddess Is
(Sung to *The King of Love My Shepherd Is*)

Alissa DeLaFuente

The heart of love my Goddess is
Whose wholeness fails me never;
I lack for nothing in light of this
And She is mine forever.

Where streams of living water flow
You carve our paths in sand and stone;
And where the verdant meadows grow
You offer cure and shelter.

Were dark and painful, oft my days
And yet in love She sought me;
Upon her bosom I gently lay
And Home, rejoining, brought me.

In death's dark vale, I fear no ill
With you, Great Mother, beside me.
Your heart and hands my comfort still,
Your warmth surrounds to guide me.

You spread a table in my sight,
Your healing balm bestowing;
And O what joy and true delight
From Your bounteous chalice flowing.

And so, through all the length of days,
Your wholeness fails me never.
Goddess, may we sing Your praise
Upon this Earth forever.

Her Eye is on the Sparrow
(Sung to *His Eye is on the Sparrow*)

Trista Hendren

Why should I feel discouraged,
Why should the shadows come,
Why should my heart be broken,
And long for a Father above?
When Goddess is my portion.
My constant Friend is She;
Her eye is on the sparrow,
And I know She watches over me.

Refrain:
I sing because I'm happy,
I sing because I'm free;
Her eye is on the sparrow,
And I know She watches over me.

"Let not your heart be troubled,"
Her tender words I hear,
And resting on Her goodness,
I lose my doubts and fears;
Though by the path She leadeth,
The steps I cannot see;
Her eye is on the sparrow,
And I know She watches over me.

Refrain:
I sing because I'm happy,
I sing because I'm free;
Her eye is on the sparrow,
And I know She watches over me.

Down in the River
Liz Childs Kelly

As I went down in the river to pray,
Oshun wash my pain away
And You who wear the robe and crown,
Oshun, show me the way.

Oh sisters, let's go down,
Let's go down, come on down,
Oh sisters, let's go down,
Down in the river to pray.

As I went down in the river to pray,
Ganga wash my troubles away
And You who hold the lily and lute,
Ganga, show me the way.

Oh mothers, let's go down,
Let's go down, come on down,
Oh mothers, let's go down,
Down in the river to pray.

As I went down in the river to pray,
Danu wash my sorrows away
And You, the Great Mother of All,
Danu, show me the way.

Oh daughters, let's go down
Let's go down, come on down,
Oh, daughters, let's go down,
Down in the river to pray.

As I went down in the river to pray,
Boann wash my cares away
And You, who calls the milk to flow,
Boann show me the way.

Oh children, let's go down
Let's go down, don't you wanna go down,
Oh, children, let's go down,
Down in the river to pray.

As I went down in the river to pray,
Vajravahari wash my fears away,
And You, who guard the sacred lands
Vajravahari show me the way.

Oh women, let's go down,
Let's go down, come on down,
Oh women, let's go down,
Down in the river to pray.

As I went down in the river to pray,
Holy Mother I honor you each day,
And You, our Great Beginning and End,
Holy Mother, show us the way.

Grey Power

Cheryl Braganza

49

Life Spirals On
(Sung to *I'll Fly Away*)
Liz Childs Kelly

Some bright morning when this body wears out
I'll spiral on
Returning to the one eternal Heart
I'll spiral on

Life spirals on, oh glory
Life spirals on, in the Mother
Love never ends, it comes back 'round again
Life spirals on

Like the old leaf falling from the tree
I'll spiral on
Returning to the Earth to feed next season's seeds
I'll spiral on

Life spirals on, oh glory
Life spirals on, in the Mother
Love never ends, it comes back 'round again
Life spirals on

Oh, how glad and happy just to breathe
I'll spiral on
Blue sky above, Mother Earth beneath my feet
I'll spiral on

Life spirals on, oh glory
Life spirals on, in the Mother
Love never ends, it comes back 'round again,
Life spirals on

Each day a gift, I feel them come and go
I'll spiral on
Surrendering all to love's eternal flow
I'll spiral on

Life spirals on, oh glory
Life spirals on, in the Mother
Love never ends, it comes back 'round again
Life spirals on

I Love to Tell the Story
Monette Chilson

I love to tell the story of unseen things within:
of Goddess in her wisdom, with no concept of sin.
I love to tell the story, because I know 'tis true.
It satisfies my longings as nothing else could do.

I love to tell her story,
Nearly lost in all its glory
to tell the old, old story
of Goddess without end.

I love to tell the story. 'Tis an honor to repeat
which seems, each time I tell it, to make me more complete.
I love to tell the story, so many have never heard
the message of reclamation in Goddess's holy word.

I love to tell her story,
Nearly lost in all its glory
to tell the old, old story
of Goddess without end.

I love to tell the story, that beats within our breast
To sprits hungering and thirsting, she alone brings rest.
And when her power fills me, I sing her ancient song,
'twill be the old, old story that my soul has known so long.

I love to tell her story,
Nearly lost in all its glory
to tell the old, old story
of Goddess without end.

I Love My Piano
Cheryl Braganza

I Love to Tell Her Story
(Sung to *I Love to Tell the Story*)
Sharon Smith

I love to tell Her story of a Mother's purest Love,
Of Goddess and Her Wisdom: within us, not "above."
I love to tell Her story, because I know that it's true;
My Womansoul bears witness, as nothing else can do.

Refrain:
I love to tell Her story,
So maligned by Patriarchy
To tell the ancient story
Of Goddess and Her love.

I love to tell Her story; more wonderful it seems
Than all the gold and jewels of those patriarchal dreams.
I love to tell Her story, it did so much for me;
To heal my woman wounds and restore my sovereignty.

(Refrain)

I love to tell Her story; empow'ring to repeat
What seems, each time I tell it, more wonderfully sweet.
I love to tell Her story, for women need to know
The message of our freedom we lost so long ago.

(Refrain)

I love to tell Her story, for those who know it best
Are fighting Patriarchy to free all the rest.
And when the chains are broken, we'll shout the Mother's song,
Of ancient Goddess Wisdom that we have loved so long.

(Refrain)

Abide with Me
Jeanine Elizabeth Otte

Abide with Me, fast falls the evening tide
The darkness deepens Goddess in me Rise
When others hear me and hold space with me
Love is renewed again, Abide with Me.

I need My Presence every passing hour.
What but deep Love can ground me in My Power?
Who but MySelf, my Queen Divine in Me
Shine in My Heart, My Voice, Abide with Me.

Swift to my gaze arrives the Black night sky
Bright moon in phases, sings with ocean tides
Changing and shifting, forms known yet unseen
Story create and tend, Abide with Me

I see my fears and name them honestly.
Anguish expressed will lighten weight, release.
Where is receding, smallness, harm, decay?
I speak in Truth; Transform; Abide with Me

Hold now My Vision with My closing eyes
Cosmos unfolding diamonds shine in skies
Sun greet me in your newness and return
In life perpetual, Abide with Me

The Old Rounded Crone
(Sung to *The Old Rugged Cross*)
Trista Hendren

On a hill far away, stood an old rounded Crone
The emblem of all we revered
And I love that old Crone who resembles me now
After decades of love and babies.

So I'll cherish the old rounded Crone
Till my shame, I at last, lay down
I will cling to the old rounded Crone
Till I learn how to love all that I am.

See they taught us to hate, any fat on ourselves
Our mothers and grandmother's shamed.
For they wanted us small, and to deal with it all
While they stole our divinity.

So I'll cherish the old rounded Crone
Till my shame, I at last, lay down
I will cling to the old rounded Crone
Till I learn how to love all that I am.

Oh, that old rounded Crone so despised by the world
Has a wondrous attraction for me
For the dear Willendorf, left Her body to love
To show us how grand we can be.

So I'll cherish the old rounded Crone
Till my shame, I at last, lay down
I will cling to the old rounded Crone
Till I learn how to love all that I am.

In the old rounded Crone, stain'd with blood so divine
A wondrous beauty I see
For she laid it all bare, without need for despair
So boldly proclaiming I AM!!

So I'll cherish the old rounded Crone
Till my shame, I at last, lay down
I will cling to the old rounded Crone
Till I learn how to love all that I am.

Now the old rounded Crone, bears my Nana's lost hopes*
She tells me there are other ways
You see long, long ago, before men had a go
Women were H-O-L-Y

So I'll cherish the old rounded Crone
Till my shame, I at last, lay down
I will cling to the old rounded Crone
Till I learn how to love all that I am.

There is never a day, I don't miss my Nano*
But in Willendorf, she I see
Then She'll call me some day to our Goddess estate
Where Her hugs I'll forever embrace!

So I'll cherish the old rounded Crone
Till my shame, I at last, lay down
I will cling to the old rounded Crone
Till I learn how to love that all I am!

Trista's re-write of *The Old Rugged Cross*, written by George Bennard in 1912
was inspired by Anique Radiant Heart's photographic description of her
beautiful journey in Austria in our *Willendorf's Legacy* anthology.

*Nana was my maternal grandmother, JoAnne, and Nano was my paternal
grandmother, Marge. While I still miss them both every day, they still come to
me often in my dreams.

Belonging

Anique Radiant Heart

Rock of Ages
Deborah Meyerriecks

Rock of Ages, support me,
As I climb my way to see;
All the vastness of Her gifts,
As I feel energy shift;
Glowing spiral, unlocked key,
Goddess Strength flowing through me.

From the mountains to the seas,
As steward, She entrusts me;
For the waters are Her blood,
And the rock is of Her bone;
Rock of Ages, support me,
Goddess Strength flowing though me.

She sustains us so we must,
Do the work, maintain the trust;
Life abundant, overflows,
Healing where intention flows;
Rock of Ages, support me,
Goddess Strength flowing though me.

Goddess whisper to my heart,
Let me know where I should start;
The work is vast, the need great,
We must begin before too late;
Rock of Ages, support me,
Goddess Strength flowing though me.

Mother Holy
(Sung to *Infant Holy*)
Jeanine Elizabeth Otte

Mother Holy
Hold Me Closely
in Your Bosom Heart Divine
Mother Holy
Deep within Me
Shine through my Heart and My Voice
Sing the chorus
Sing the minor
Sing the major harmonies
Mother Holy Songs of You
Mother Holy Songs of Me

Tree most Holy
Rootly grounded
with Your branches curved and holding
Tree most Holy
Spinning spirals
through cosmic mystery
Sun Star magnetizing energy
flowing through you and Me
Tree Most Holy
Oldly Shine
Earth Most Holy
Cosmic Thine

Lover Holy
Walking Slowly
Speaking Strongly in Your Voice
Lover Holy
softly sleeping
loving Me in every breath
Exploring deeply the sorrows buried
for your Heart first and for Mine
Lover Holy, My Divine
Lover Holy We Divine

Infant Holy Star Shine Sparkling
Light You are and All and All
Infant Holy Sun Child Wisdom
Teach Me with Your Artful being
In your questions
and your pleading
and your holding
and your loving
Infant Holy
Lion Mine
Infant Holy
Joy Divine

Daughter Holy
Fire Inside You
burning red rage and desire
Dragon rising with voice reclaiming
generations evermore
Skin recoiling nerves ascending
life blood loosen and Truth releasing
Holy Daughter
Queen Divine
Holy Daughter
All Divine

Sister Holy hold me loosely as I walk on my path
Sister Holy hold me softly as you watch me start a way
Goddess ever leading me with great Spirit ever glowing
Goddess now alive in me
Goddess now alive in me

I most Holy
Hold I inward as I quiet, deepen sight
I most Holy
Inner darkness shining Queen with staff so bright
Doe enlightening, Owl watching,
Lioness roaring, Humpbacks dancing
I most Holy
All Am I
I most Holy
I Divine

Dear Goddess Mother of us all
(Sung to *Dear Lord and Father of Mankind*)

Kay Louise Aldred

Dear Goddess Mother of us all,
Ignite our playful ways!
Stimulate Sophia's sight,
So, we may vision paths of Light,
And the radiance of your ways
The beauty of your gaze.

Through devotion the Priestess heard
The calling of the Land.
Inspired by whispers on the wind,
She rose and drummed and began to sing,
The story of the Earth
The wisdom of the Earth

The flames of Eros lick, caress
And stimulate the womb,
Creatrix fire of women's blood
Warms the whole being, head to foot,
And through this we birth anew,
We co-create with you.

Goddess Gaia grounds and holds,
We praise her stable force!
Her seasons mirror, guide, and show
Our feminine cycles help us grow,
 As we know we'll die again,
And then we'll rise again.

The moving waters of Ancient Wells
Hold all the codes of health,
Let us revere and honour flux,
Reclaiming Sacred Womanhood!
And the sanctuary of flow,
Which originates below.

Breathe through the Sacred Heart desires
Our Dragon lifeforce power!
Revive divinity of flesh,
Speak through the pleasure we possess!
In every Sacred cell,
This story we retell.

The Healing Circle
Sue Ellen Parkinson

Because She Lives
(Sung to *Because He Lives*)
Monette Chilson

Goddess in bloom, the true apostle;
She came to love, heal and align;
She lived and died, Magdalene revealed
A heart so pure is there to prove my beloved lives!

Chorus
Because She lives, I can face tomorrow,
Because She lives, all fear is gone;
Because I know She lives on in me,
And life is worth the living,
Just because She lives!

How sweet to nurse a newborn baby,
And feel the holy cord that binds;
But greater still the calm assurance:
This child can face uncertain days because She Lives!

Chorus
Because She lives, I can face tomorrow,
Because She lives, all fear is gone;
Because I know She lives on in me,
And life is worth the living,
Just because She lives!

And then one day, I'll cross the river,
Her many faces will appear;
Durga, Sophia and sweet Magdalena
I'll feel the light within me and I'll know She lives!

Chorus
Because She lives, I can face tomorrow,
Because She lives, all fear is gone;
Because I know she lives within me,
And life is worth the living,
Just because She lives!

The Magdalene's my Guide, I Shall not Want
(Sung to *The Lord's My Shepherd*)
Kay Louise Aldred

The Magdalene's my Guide, I shall not want;
she spirals me deep inside,
through rainbow streams; she leadeth me,
to ignite my wisdom fires.

My soul she doth restore again,
the Queendom walk I make,
down regal paths of sovereignty,
my Goddess empowerment wakes.

My body she has glorified,
defying the male gaze,
the mound of Venus fountain flows,
as Eros flames blaze.

Devotion. Desire. They ground my life,
the Feminine she moves as me,
the living, blooming, blood red rose,
my dwelling place shall be.

The Magdalene's my Guide, I shall not want;
she spirals me deep inside,
through rainbow streams; she leadeth me,
and ignites my wisdom fires.

The Mystic Mary Magdalene
Sue Ellen Parkinson

We Give Our Thanks to Her
(Sung to *Now Thank We All Our God*)
Rebekah Myers

We give our thanks to Her
Our Goddess, most exalted,
Who wondrous works hath made,
Who is our best belovéd
Who from Her Mother-arms
Hath blessed us on our way
With countless gifts of love,
That still are ours today.

O may our Goddess bright
Through all our life be near us,
And with Her pow'r and might
Give peace and joy to cheer us,
And keep us in Her grace
And comfort us when dismayed,
And free us from all ills
To make us unafraid

All praise and thanks to Her,
The Mother, now be given,
Who is our gracious Queen
Amid the highest heaven –
Our Mother strong and good
Whom earth and heaven adore;
For thus it was and is
And shall be evermore.
Amen.

Traditional Hymn adapted by Rebekah Myers
Copyright © August 16, 2021 by Rebekah Myers

Be Still and Know that I am You
(Sung to *Be Still and Know that I am God*)

Kay Louise Aldred

Be still and know that I am in You,
Be still and know that I am of You,
Be still and know that I am You.

I am the Flow, that healeth thee,
I am the Pleasure, that healeth thee,
I am the Rest, that healeth thee.

In thee, oh Body, I put my trust,
In thee, Instinct, I put my trust,
In thee, my Knowing, I put my trust.

Be Still, For the Presence of Goddess
(Sung to *Be Still, For the Presence of the Lord*)
Dr. Lynne Sedgmore

Be still, feel the presence of Goddess, Her sacredness is here,
Sit down beside Her now, and feel her close and dear.
In Her our truth is found, She is our holy ground.
Be still, feel the presence of Goddess, Her sacredness is here.

Be still, for the power of Goddess is flowing through us all,
She burns the holy flame, Her Sovereignty unfurled.
Shining through day and night, our radiant Queen of light.
Be still, for the power of Goddess is flowing through us all.

Be still, Goddess energy and love are moving through our hearts.
Her waters clean and heal, Her air the breath of grace,
Her body is the land, on Her we live and stand.
Be still, Goddess energy and love are moving through our hearts.

From the Garden
(Sung to *In the Garden*)
Sharon Smith

I fled from the Garden today
Feeling small and somewhat appalling;
Then a voice so clear
Sounded in my ear
The voice of Lilith calling:

"Come and walk with me
Claim your Sovereignty,
It's your right, by Goddess decree!
Feel your joy renewed,
Patriarchy's screwed:
Eat your fill of the Fruit of the Tree!"

Lilith spoke and She
told me the Truth
Of the Goddess and Matriarchy;
And Her Wisdom Song
carried me along,
far from Patriarchy.

Now She walks with me,
Lilith talks to me,
Tells me not to bow to Man's Throne:
I belong to no man,
I'm not "lesser than,"
I'm a Goddess all on my own.

I belong to no man,
I'm not "lesser than"...
I'm a Goddess all on my own!

Lilith
Arna Baartz

Lilith Paid It All
(Sung to *Jesus Paid It All*)
Sharon Smith

Verse 1

I hear the Goddess say,
"Your life indeed is small;
Child of Patriarchy, pray,
Look to Lilith, heed Her call."

Refrain:
Lilith paid it all,
Defying God's decree,
All to Her I owe,
She brought me Sovereignty.

Verse 2

Lilith, now indeed I find
Your power in saying No
Has changed all Women's lives
And given us strength to grow.

(Refrain)

Verse 3

For nothing good can come
From God as "He" in three
Which has held us all in chains
Since Eve first bent her knee.

(Refrain)

Verse 4

Now when before the SHE,
I stand in Her complete,
"Lilith taught me to be free,"
My lips will still repeat.

Refrain:
Lilith paid it all,
Defying God's decree
All to Her I owe,
She brought me Sovereignty.

We Gather Together

Carol P. Christ

We gather together to ask for your blessing
And if you are willing, our hearts to make whole.
The Goddess is with us among our offerings
She gladly takes to Her the gifts that we bring.

Shared with permission.

Five Sisters Unite

Cheryl Braganza

Goddess We Adore You
(Sung *To God Be the Glory*)

Dr Lynne Sedgmore

Goddess we adore you,
Your presence we feel,
Your deep love restores,
And our goodness reveals.
You offer abundance
From your fertile earth,
You want us to know
Our own truth and our worth.

Hail Goddess! Hail Goddess!
As we walk on your lands,
Hail Goddess! Hail Goddess!
As we raise up our hands.
You are our dear Mother,
The Birther of all,
Goddess we adore you
May all hear your call.

Let's feed every person,
All cherish Gaia,
Protect all our waters,
The earth, air and fire.
We grow through your grace,
We always have choice.
Your blessings restore us,
We sing with one voice.

Hail Goddess! Hail Goddess!
As we walk on your lands,
Hail Goddess! Hail Goddess!
As we raise up our hands.
You are our dear Mother,
The Birther of all,
Goddess we adore you
May all hear your call.

You teach us the wisdom
And power of your ways,
To know, love and serve you
The rest of our days.
Yet deeper and higher
Your presence can be.
You release our light
And creativity.

Hail Goddess! Hail Goddess!
As we walk on your lands,
Hail Goddess! Hail Goddess!
As we raise up our hands.
You are our dear Mother,
The Birther of all,
Goddess we adore you
May all hear your call.

Hail Goddess! Hail Goddess!
As we walk on your lands,
Hail Goddess! Hail Goddess!
As we raise up our hands.
You are our dear Mother,
The Birther of all,
Goddess we adore you
May all hear your call.

How Great Thou Art

Trista Hendren

Oh Asherah
When I, in awesome wonder
Consider all the worlds Thy hands have made
I see the stars, I hear the rolling thunder
Thy power throughout the universe displayed

Then sings my soul, my Goddess always be
How great Thou art, how great Thou art
Then sings my soul, my Goddess always be
How great Thou art, how great Thou art

And when I think of how we've burnt your body
Forgot your name, I scarce can take it in
Despite it all, you were here boldly claiming
You birthed us all, through You we're all akin.

Then sings my soul, my Goddess always be
How great Thou art, how great Thou art
Then sings my soul, my Goddess always be
How great Thou art, how great Thou art

When you arise, with loving acclamation
Our hearts awake, and joy will fill us all.
Then we all rise, in glorious adorations
And there proclaim, Goddess, how great Thou art

Then sings my soul, my Goddess always be
How great Thou art, how great Thou art
Then sings my soul, my Goddess always be
How great Thou art, how great Thou art

Song Birds

Cheryl Braganza

Earth, She is our Mother
(Sung to *This is My Father's World*)

Deborah A. Meyerriecks

Earth, She is our Mother
With Us She shares her gifts
Nature flow-s, Magic Grow-s
The face of Gaia shows
Earth, She is our Mother
I thrive within the thought
Of rocks and trees, of skies and seas
Her love these wonders have brought.

Earth She is our Mother
Mother to Sky as well,
Animal, element, and plant
Earth She is our Mother
By land and sea and sky
By Spirit through mind's eye
Wise, She whispers within our hearts
Of the Magick of love we share.

Earth She is our Mother
From Her we received life
With love we give her our respect
Our magic realized
Earth, She is our Mother
Abundance overflows
To those who give and not just take
Gaia's Blessings She bestows

I Surrender All
Pat Daly

Mother Goddess I surrender,
All to you I freely give;
I will ever love and trust you,
In your presence daily live.

Refrain:
I surrender all,
I surrender all,
All to thee, dear blessed Goddess,
I surrender all.

Mother Goddess I surrender,
Humbly at your feet I bow,
Patriarchy all forsaken,
Take me, Mother, take me now.

(Refrain)

Mother Goddess I surrender;
Hold me in your sweet embrace
Let your spirit move me Mother
As I gaze upon your face.

(Refrain)

Mother Goddess I surrender,
Yes, I give myself to thee,
Fill me with thy love and power,
Let thy blessings cover me.

(Refrain)

All to Goddess I surrender;
No more do I feel ashamed.
Oh, the joy of full acceptance!
Glory, glory, to her name!

(Refrain)

Salvatrix Mundi
Lisbeth Cheever-Gessaman

"In God is a woman like yourself." -Carol P. Christ

Blessed Assurance

Trista Hendren

Blessed assurance, Goddess is mine
Oh, what a foretaste of healing divine
Emancipation, running from God
Born of Her spirit, washed in Her blood

This is my story, this is my song
Loving my Goddess all the day long
This is my story, this is my song
Loving my Goddess all the day long

You have restored me, all is at rest
I in my Goddess, am happy and blessed
In meditation, looking within
Filled with Her kindness, blessed with Her love

This is my story, this is my song
Loving my Goddess all the day long
This is my story, this is my song
Loving my Goddess all the day long

I am Worthy

(Sung to the tune of the children's hymn, *Jesus Loves Me*)

Michelle Kathleen Elder

I am worthy, this I know,
For my body tells me so.
Everyone like me belongs;
When I'm weak, and when I'm strong.

Yes, I am worthy!
Yes, I am worthy!
Yes, I am worthy!
My body tells me so.

Magdalene Blessing Womankind

Sue Ellen Parkinson

Sweet Hour of Prayer

Trista Hendren and Sharon Smith

1 Sweet hour of prayer; Sweet hour of prayer,
that calls me from a world of care,
and brings me to my Mother's home
make all my wants and wishes known.

In seasons of distress and grief,
my soul has often found relief,
And oft escaped the world's despair
by thy return, sweet hour of prayer!

2 Sweet hour of prayer; sweet hour of prayer,
I find my consolation there;
With She whose mothering heart, I know,
Will healing bring to our Womansoul.

With such I hasten to the place
where Goddess now will show Her face,
and gladly take my station there,
and wait for Her, sweet hour of prayer!

3 Sweet hour of prayer; sweet hour of prayer,
Take all my shame, and my burdens bear
On wings of Love to my Mother's heart
And gratefulness to Her now impart.

And since She longs to show Her face,
believe Her love, and trust Her grace,
I'll share with Her my every care,
and wait for thee, sweet hour of prayer!

Lovingly, Clearly
(Sung to *Softly and Tenderly*)
Liz Childs Kelly

Lovingly, clearly the Goddess is calling –
Calling to you and to me
Never been silenced, She's always been present
Waiting for you and for me!

Come home, come home
You who are sacred come home!
Lovingly, clearly Our Mother, She calls us
Calling, Oh, Daughters, come home!

Life never ending, Her love all around us
Enfolding you and me,
Nothing to fear, Her body surrounds us
Here for you and for me!

Come home, come home
You who are sacred come home!
Lovingly, clearly Our Mother, She calls us
Calling, Oh, Daughters, come home!

Why remain silent when Goddess is with us,
Walking with you and with me?
Why should we linger and not stand beside Her?
She stands with you and with me!

Come home, come home
You who are sacred come home!
Lovingly, clearly Our Mother. She calls us
Calling, Oh, Daughters, come home!

Oh, for the wonderful love that She gives us
Love that's for you and for me,
Wisdom upon us, showered in blessings,
Blessings for you and for me!

Come home, come home
You who are sacred come home!
Lovingly, clearly Our Mother. She calls us
Calling, Oh, Daughters, come home!

Harper

Andrea Redmond

Lift up the Veil

(Sung to *Praise to the Lord, the Almighty*)

Deborah A. Meyerriecks

Lift up the Veil, see to within,
The Liminal Surrounding
Here in this space, perceive Her face,
Goddess Persephone.
Maiden of Spring, Demeter's Child transformed,
Herself into Death's Sovereign Queen.

She bears the truth, each seed must die,
in order to bear life's fruit.
At Summer's End, Journey again,
back home to partner and throne.
Go deep within, Shed what no longer can serve,
during your long night of the soul.

Poison or cure, we've but to learn,
Lessons from life's experience
Kore rules shade, Her garden thrives,
from shadow back into the light.
Lessons we learn, sow patience and trust within,
with pruning and resting we thrive

Boundaries intact, Limits in place,
Lessons run deep as the Night
Embrace your death and truly live,
Release what no longer serves
Bringer of Death and our regeneration,
Guide us to know our true selves

Lift up the Veil, see to within,
The Liminal Surrounding
Here in this space, now see your face,
Eyes glow with personal knowing
Your life transformed, by strength of your divine will,
Now journey back home to yourself.

Is The Morrigan Calling to you?
(Sung to *All Creatures of Our God and King!*)

Deborah A. Meyerriecks

Across night's shadow see Her form
Goddess' voice makes itself known
Is The Morrigan? Calling to you?
Ravens and crows are taking wing
Sovereign Queens with warrior strength
The Sovereign daughters of Ernmas
Anu, Macha and Badb

Soft, voices call upon the wind,
Sovereign of Land and Sea and Sky.
Hear The Morrigan, Calling to you.
Land that nourishes and provides
Warrior Steward called to Her side
Protecting health of Land, though voice and Deed
For Anu, Anand, An Morrigan,

Lift up the Sword She gives to you
Fighting when the cause is just
Thus The Morrigan, has called to you.
Red Haired Queen of Sovereignty
Warrior Queen! Lady of the Sidhe!
Invoking peace, at the battles end,
Macha, may we always be friends, never foes.

Battle crow with Frenzied Madness,
Dance on spear point, haze of battle
Dark Phantom Queen, weaver of fate
Red-Mouthed Badb, Washer at the Ford,
Open our eyes to see our truth.
Badb's waters cleanse me, Empty and fill me.
Lady of Magick, flowing through time, Life, death and rebirth.

Magic and Mystery: Answering Her Call

Arlene Bailey

In the Shadow Before Dawn
(Sung to *For the Beauty of the Earth*)

Deborah A. Meyerriecks

In the Shadow before Dawn,
Before sunlight fills the skies
Whispers heard upon the night
Of the Truth within us lies

With Goddess, we find our strength
Authenticity with grace

Empow'r us to see our truth
So much more than what we see
In the midnight hours we learn
That which we would choose to be

With Goddess, we find our strength
Authenticity with grace

Under Moon and Stars so bright
Magic goes like water flows
As the day turns into night
Nourish us so we may grow

With Goddess, we find our strength
Authenticity with grace

With each day we start anew
We look within and truly see
With our work, we continue
Seek to know through prophesy

With Goddess, we find our strength
Authenticity with grace

LES SIRENNES
Claire Dorey

Support My Quest To Know Myself
(Sung to *Praise My Soul The King Of Heaven*)

Deborah A. Meyerriecks

Support my quest to know myself
Goddess guide my journey home.
Searching through the shadowed darkness
Through the long night of the soul.
Battered, Beaten, yet far from done
Poured out, emptied and refilled.

Learning to give myself some grace
Learning life is not a race.
After a fall I will stand
Goddess takes me by the hand.
Seeking, knowing, yearning, learning
Each step closer to myself

Torch Bearer mark where I came from
As I find my way back home.
Unlearn the parts that aren't me
Accept my sovereignty.
Restoring and Reclaiming me!
Shining light that I can see.

Digging, searching, and enduring
Solace found within the knowing.
Spiral within to liminal space
Divine within mortal space.
As above then so below.
As the Universe, so the soul

On my journey to know Goddess
Finding Her within myself
Spiral path illuminated
Journey outward from within
Standing ready for my journey
One step inward to begin.

LES SIRENNES IV

Claire Dorey

Be Thou My Vision[12]

Barbara O'Meara

Be Thou my Vision, O Goddess of my heart;
Naught be all else to me, save that Thou art.
Thou my best Thought, by day or by night,
Waking or sleeping, Thy presence my light.

Be Thou my Wisdom, and Thou my true Word;
I ever with Thee, my Divine Feminine,
Thou my great Mother, I Thy true daughter;
Thou in me dwelling, and I with Thee one.

Be Thou my battle Shield, Sword for the fight;
Be Thou my Dignity, Thou my Delight;
Thou my soul's Shelter, Thou my high Tow'r:
Raise all Sacred Sisters to the highest of power.

Riches I heed not, nor any man's empty praise,
Thou mine Inheritance, now and always:
Thou and Thou only, first in my heart,
High Priestess Universal, my Treasure Thou art.

High Priestess Universal, my victory is well won,
May I reach divine awakening, O Aine, bright Sun!
Heart of my heart aligned to Rhiannon's Full Moon
Be thou my everlasting Vision, O Goddess Universal.

---

12 6th or 8th Century Irish Celtic Hymn.

Serenity in Shekinah
(Sung to *Victory in Jesus*)
Monette Chilson

I heard an old, old story of Shekinah deep within us,
How She gave us breath within our breast to revive a soul like me.
I heard about Her groaning, Her precious blood shed birthing.
To place Herself within our hearts, so we could clearly see.

O breath of life, Shekinah, my indwelling forever,
She sought me and taught me that I was Her beloved;
She loved me ere I knew Her, and all my love is due Her,
She awakened my divinity with Her breath, a cleansing flood.

I heard about Her healing, of Her cleansing power revealing.
How She made the lame to walk again and caused the blind to see;
And then I cried, "Shekinah, be with my broken spirit,"
Shekinah breathed within me and brought me serenity.

O breath of life, Shekinah, my indwelling forever,
She sought me and taught me that I was Her beloved;
She loved me ere I knew Her, and all my love is due Her,
She awakened my divinity with Her breath, a cleansing flood.

I heard about Her simple life so pure and full of glory
And I heard about the soothing calm so like the crystal sea;
About the angels singing and the old redemptive story,
Both here and there, I'll sing Her song of sweet serenity.

O breath of life, Shekinah, my indwelling forever,
She sought me and taught me that I was Her beloved;
She loved me ere I knew Her, and all my love is due Her,
She awakened my divinity with Her breath, a cleansing flood.

Procession to the Goddess Ériu
Barbara O' Meara

Mother Goddess, We Adore Thee
(Sung to *Joyful, Joyful We Adore Thee*)

Sharon Smith

Mother Goddess, we adore You,
Evermore Creatrix be;
Maiden, Mother, Crone before us,
Let us hail the Triple Three.

First the Maiden, Sweet as Springtime
Then the Mother, Life's first Breath;
Last, the Crone in Wisdom shrouded,
Standing at the Gate of Death.

Mother Goddess, we implore You,
Teach us of Your Earthly Ways,
Sun and Stars and Moon around us,
Cycle of unbroken days.

Field and forest, vale and mountain,
Flowery meadow, full of dew
Singing bird and flowing river
Call us to remember You.

You're the Loving, Giving Mother
Ever blessing, ever blest,
Wellspring of the joy of living,
Ocean depth of happy rest!

Both our Mother and our Sister,
Hail the Goddess, the Great SHE!
Teach us how to live and love
In Nature's sacred Harmony.

Women, join the happy chorus,
Which the morning stars began;
Mother love rains down upon us,
As we gather hand-in-hand.

Ever dancing 'neath the Moonlight,
Daughters of the Mystery;
Her sweet music keeps us singing
Of Her praises, Blessed be!

Faith of Our Mothers
(Sung to *Faith of Our Fathers*)
Sharon Smith

Faith of our Mothers, living still,
In spite of dungeon, fire, and sword;
Beaten and tortured, imprisoned and starved,
All for the Goddess they loved and adored.
Faith of our Mothers, Wild and Free:
We'll honor it always! Blessed be!

Our Mothers, dancing beneath a Full Moon,
Honored the Earth; Her cycles embraced,
Devoted to Goddess, they followed Her ways,
Through the Hangings and Burning they often faced.
Faith of our Mothers, Wild and Free:
We'll honor it always! Blessed be!

Faith of our Mothers, we'll not forget,
'Twas judged and condemned by Church decree;
Labeled as Witches and Women Unclean
Still they stood strong in their Sovereignty!
Faith of our Mothers, Wild and Free:
We'll honor it always! Blessed be!

Hear us, O Mothers, we now pledge our love
To the Great SHE of whom Nature sings;
Nevermore bending a trembling knee
To a male Trinity or his earthly kings!
Faith of our Mothers, Wild and Free:
We'll honor it always! Blessed be!

Faith of our Mothers, Wild and Free:
We'll honor it always! Blessed be!

Praise Goddess
(Sung to *Doxology*)
Kate Hilderbrandt

Praise Goddess, mystery unknown
Praise she who birthed the world we know
Her gifts in great abundance flow
Praise Goddess: mother, maiden, crone

Praise Her from Whom All Blessings Flow
Carol P. Christ

Praise Her from whom all blessings flow
Praise Her all creatures here below
Praise Her above in wings of flight
Praise Her in darkness and in light.

Shared with permission.

Women Rising

Barbara O' Meara

Singing our Way to Freedom

Trista Hendren

I have tried to raise my children the opposite of how I was. That said, even among feminists, having a daughter who is loud, proud and unashamed is often frowned upon. Truth be told, many still prefer the silent and tame models when it comes to females.

Last night, I was baking Christmas cookies with Helani and my favorite Christmas song came on the radio. I re-wrote it several times with my husband, and the softer version will be printed in our upcoming Solstice Carol Book. (The funny version is just for close friends!) I realized upon hearing the original version of *O Holy Night* that I had, perhaps, succeeded in raising my daughter as I intended.

The questions that arose from a critical listening of that untouched writing revealed a daughter who had not been tainted by the shame of church teachings.

> *What is he saving us from, mom?*
> *But, why would we need a savior?...*

Indeed we do not. Most of us were served a load of crap. And in our need to be 'good' girls, we ate it all up—despite the stomach pains.

It's time for more nourishing food.

We must begin to see ourselves as the Goddesses that we are. We must begin to experience our bodies—and our blood—as holy.

I shared these lines from Ntozake Shange in my first book, which I wrote for my daughter in hopes that she would find herself in the Divine.[13]

> *we need a god who bleeds now*
> *whose wounds are not the end of anything*[14]

I leave them here again in hopes that those of us who grew up with the shame narrative can also leave it in the dust.

I am often haunted by the words of Andrea Dworkin, but none so much as this one sentence. After decades of searching, I am still not sure I know the answer.

"What would freedom be for us?"[15]

I have spent many hours debating this question with circle sisters. None of us has ever known where to even begin to answer it.

I hope it does not take me the rest of my life to answer this for myself. I am grateful to know that our work as Goddess feminists has shown our daughters and granddaughters a shortcut through the nonsense. That said, I wish I had found this path sooner.

I am no longer an evangelical—even about Goddess. I don't have that same fervency I once did to convince people to join my way of thinking. People find Goddess in their own way or time. (Or they don't.)

No one is going to "hell." She loves us all—Just as we are.

---

13 Hendren, Trista. *The Girl God*. Girl God Books; 2012.

14 Shange, Ntozake. *For Colored Girls Who Have Considered Suicide When the Rainbow Is Enuf.* Scribner; 1997.

15 Dworkin, Andrea. *Life and Death*. Free Press; 2002.

I hope the singing of these new words will be deeply healing—
both individually and collectively.

Be sure to join us for our Zoom sing-alongs—and by all means,
please sing these songs in your local community as well when you
are able.

May we all find the freedom that is our birthright.

List of Contributors

Alissa DeLaFuente lives and works in the Pacific Northwest. Her fiction, nonfiction, and poetry have appeared in scientific and literary journals, including *Gold Man Review*, *Red Savina Review*, and others. In response to the pandemic, she wrote and self-published a book on time management and gentle goal-setting to help young people manage the chaos. It came out in May 2020, and is titled *Get Your Life Together: A practical guide to getting organized*. She regularly serves as a prose judge for the International Latino Book Awards. Visit her at www.alissadelafuente.com to learn more.

Andrea Redmond has been a feminist rights activist, artist and pagan for over 50 years. She has been a devotee of The Morrigan since a young girl.

She was born on Prince Edward Island, Canada of Irish descent and moved to Ireland with her young family and there, she was one of the first women in Belfast to paint wall murals. Her first mural in 1983 honoured women's rights activists from Ireland and South Africa. She has painted over 40 murals with similar themes and her work has been featured in a number of publications and films on Northern Ireland.

She has worked and chaired a number of women's, art and multicultural groups. She has taught programs in art, community development and youth work. She is a mother to three children and returned to education in her 40s, completing her PhD, at the University of Ulster.

Andrea currently resides in rural Donegal, Ireland where she operates her art studio/workshop. Her artwork is in permanent collections and galleries in Ireland, Canada and the United States.

Anique Radiant Heart is High Priestess of the Global Goddess, Goddess Scholar, Sacred Singer Songwriter, author of *Chanting the Chakras – A Way to the Goddess Through Energetic Use of Voice* and *The 33 Teachings of Kuan Yin"* – and an internationally acclaimed Spiritual Teacher. Anique Radiant Heart is a well loved member of the International Goddess Community.

A wise crone now at 73—for the past 43 years, Anique has created CDs of original music celebrating the Goddess, produced Goddess festivals, conferences, and led tours to sacred sites all over the world. In 2007, she was crowned a Foremother of the Australian Goddess Community at the Australian Goddess Conference. In 2010, she manifested the Temple of the Global Goddess for all to enjoy, and began teaching a 3-year Priestess Training program in the Temple of the Global Goddess in Maitland. Today, there are 2 Temples of the Global Goddess – the Mother House in Maitland and the Sister House in Sydney. She now has a dedicated grove of ordained Priestesses with another round of training which began in 2017. Anique has organized Goddess Conferences and Festivals in Australia since 1996, and for the past 4 years has been the co-visionary with respected Aboriginal Elder Bilawara Lee of the Australian Goddess Conference – the first conference ever in Australia to be held by an Aboriginal and Non-Aboriginal sister.

In 2017, at the Glastonbury Goddess Conference, Anique revealed and launched her Vision for an International Priestess Convocation, to take place in Crete in 2020. This gathering is designed to put into place strategies to bring about the unfolding of The Motherworld – a platform for social, political and spiritual change in the world. Dedicated to assisting women to reclaim their natural spiritual authority, Anique continues to teach women the power and joy that comes from a sacred path which celebrates the Divine Feminine. For the last 25 years, she has travelled for 3 months each year to share her teachings and music with daughters and sons of the Goddess all over the world.

http://goddess.net.au/

Arlene Bailey is a visionary artist and author working in the realm of the Sacred Female in all her many visages. Arlene's paintings and poetry/prose reflect the raw, visceral and sacred wild in all women, while challenging and questioning everything we know to be true about *the who* of who we are as women walking in this time.

Through her magical weavings in word and paint—and, drawing on her trainings and skills as an Ordained Priestess, Women's Mysteries Facilitator, Wise Woman Herbalist, Energy Medicine Practitioner and Retired Anthropologist—Arlene invites women to step into personal sovereignty as they listen to their ancient memories and voice of their soul.

Published in several Girl God Books' anthologies, Arlene is also a monthly contributor to *Return to Mago* E-Magazine and has writings in two forthcoming Mago anthologies. Her work can also be found on *The Sacred Wild*, a page on Facebook about re-wilding woman's soul.

Along with her partner and five cats, this Wild Crone lives on 18 acres of deep woods and quartz outcroppings in the Uwharrie Mountains of North Carolina, USA.

www.facebook.com/sacredwildstudio
www.instagram.com/arlenebaileyartist
www.magobooks.com
www.magoism.net

Arna Baartz is a painter, writer/poet, martial artist, educator and mother to eight fantastic children. She has been expressing herself creatively for more than 40 years and finds it to be her favourite way of exploring her inner being enough to evolve positively in an externally-focused world. Arna's artistic and literary expression is her creative perspective of the stories she observes playing out around her. Claims to fame: Arna has been selected for major art prizes and won a number of awards, published many books, and—

(her favourite) was being used as a 'paintbrush' at the age of two by well-known Australian artist John Olsen. Arna lives and works from her bush studio in the Northern Rivers, NSW Australia. Her website is www.artofkundalini.com.

Barbara O'Meara is a published writer, co-editor of *Soul Seers Irish Anthology of Celtic Shamanism*, and a professional visual artist. She has recently illustrated *My Name is Brigid* by Jessica Johnson, published by Girl God Books.

Exhibitions include 'B.O.R.N. -Babies of Ravaged Nations', group shows Lockhart Gallery New York & 'The Drawing Box' Europe, America, Far East & 'Herstory' Brigids of the World & Black Lives Matter.

Community projects i.e., 'Stitched With Love' Tuam Baby Blanket laid over the burial site at the Mother & Child Home, shown at KOLO International Women's Non Killing Cross Borders Summit in Sarajevo held by Bosnian women survivors. She is continually developing empowering women's 'Art as Activism' events i.e., 'Sort Our Smears' Campaign at 'Festival of Feminisms'.
Her Collections include: Microsoft, ESB, Dept Foreign Affairs, Irish Life, Impact Trade Union, Bologna District Council, Behaviour & Attitudes.

A recent art review stated: "Barbara O'Meara's recent paintings dealing with home and Covid are extremely beautiful and extremely coherent in their communication. Rarely is it seen where painting is used to convey complex emotional human conditions." www.barbaraomearaartist.com

Carol P. Christ (1945-2021) died peacefully on July 14 from cancer. Carol was and will remain one of the foremothers and most brilliant voices of the Women's Spirituality movement. At the conference on "The Great Goddess Re-Emerging" at the University of California at Santa Cruz in the spring of 1978, Carol delivered the keynote address, "Why Women Need the Goddess:

Phenomenological, Psychological, and Political Reflections." Christ proposed four compelling reasons why women might turn to the Goddess: the affirmation and legitimation of female power as beneficent; affirmation of the female body and its life cycles; affirmation of women's will; and affirmation of women's bonds with one another and their positive female heritage (Christ 1979).

Carol graduated from Yale University with a PhD in Religious Studies and went on to teach as a feminist scholar of women and religion, women's spirituality, and Goddess studies, at institutions including Columbia University, Harvard Divinity School, Pomona College, San Jose State University, and the California Institute of Integral Studies, where she was an adjunct professor since the inception of the Women's Spirituality, Philosophy and Religion graduate studies program in 1993. Christ published eight profoundly thoughtful and inspiring books, several in collaboration with her friend and colleague Judith Plaskow, whom she met at Yale:

- *Diving Deep and Surfacing: Women Writers on Spiritual Quest* (1986)
- *Woman Spirit Rising: A Feminist Reader in Religion*, anthology co-edited with Judith Plaskow (1992)
- *Odyssey with the Goddess: A Spiritual Quest in Crete* (1995)
- *Weaving the Visions: New Patterns in Feminist Spirituality. Anthology* co-edited with Judith Plaskow (1989)
- *Laughter of Aphrodite: Reflections on a Journey to the Goddess* (1987)
- *Rebirth of the Goddess: Finding Meaning in Feminist Spirituality* (1998)
- *She Who Changes: Re-imaging the Divine in the World* (2004)
- *Goddess and God in the World: Conversations in Embodied Theology.* Co-authored with Judith Plaskow (2016)

Christ's first book, about women writers on spiritual quest, is a book of spiritual feminist literary criticism that focused on feminist authors Kate Chopin, Margaret Atwood, Doris Lessing, Adriene Rich, and Ntozake Shange. She discovers four key aspects to women's spiritual quest: the experience of nothingness; awakening (to the powers that are greater than oneself, often found in nature); insight (into the meaning of one's life); and a new naming (in one's own terms). She emphasizes the importance of telling women's stories in order to move beyond the stories told about women by the male-centered patriarchy. Her concluding chapter speaks of a "Culture of Wholeness," that encompasses women's quest for wholeness, and she adds that, for this wholeness to be realized, the personal spiritual quest needs to be combined with the quest for social justice.

After first travelling to Greece in 1981 with the Aegean Women's Studies Institute led by her friend Ellen Boneparth, Carol fell in love with the country. She chose to live in Greece, first in Molivos on the beautiful island of Lesbos, and then moving recently to Heraklion, Crete. She had a passion for saving the environment and was active in the Green movement in Greece. she also had a love for swimming in the Aegean and sharing Greek food and wine with friends in Greece and from overseas.

Carol's fascination with Crete, ancient and modern, led her to found the Ariadne Institute for the Study of Myth and Ritual, through which she offered an educational tour, "Pilgrimage to the Goddess" twice annually. These tours introduced many to a direct experience of the ancient Earth Mother Goddess in Crete (goddessariadne.org).

In her most recent article, for the *Encyclopedia of Women in World Religion: Faith and Culture*, Christ wrote about the Goddess religion and culture of her beloved island of Crete, and the roles women played in that "egalitarian matriarchal" civilization. Her eloquent words speak not only to the Goddess religion of ancient

Crete, but also to the spirituality and ethical values she also cherished, which are much needed in our own culture today.

> "As discerners and guardians of the mysteries, women created rituals to celebrate the Source of Life and to pass the secrets of agriculture, pottery, and weaving down through the generations. The major rituals of the agricultural cycle involved blessing the seeds before planting, offering the first fruits of the harvest to the Goddess, and sharing the bounty of the harvest in communal feasts. These rituals establish that life is a gift of the Goddess and institute gift-giving as a cultural practice. As women controlled the secrets of agriculture, it makes sense that land was held by maternal clans, that kinship and inheritance passed through the maternal line, and that governance and decision-making for the group were in the hands of the elders of the maternal clan. In this context, the intelligence, love, and generosity of mothers and clan mothers would have been understood to reflect the intelligence, love, and generosity of the Goddess."[16]

Christ's Obituary was written by Mara Lynn Keller, PhD and Ellen Boneparth, who encouraged sharing.

Carolyn Lee Boyd is a writer, student drummer, and herb and native plant gardener. Her essays, short stories, memoirs, reviews, and poetry have been published in, among others, *Feminism and Religion, Return to Mago E-Magazine, Sagewoman, The Goddess Pages, Matrifocus, The Beltane Papers*, and various anthologies. She would love for you to visit her at her website, www.goddessinateapot.com where you can find some of her free e-books to download.

---

16 Carol P. Christ, "Crete, Religion and Culture" Encyclopedia of *Women in World Religions: Faith and Culture across History* [2 volumes] edited by Susan de-Gaia | Nov 16, 2018 ABC-Clio Santa Barbara 2019.

Cheryl Braganza (February 25, 1945 – December 16, 2016) was a gifted artist and poet. Of Goan origin, she was born in Bombay and grew up in Lahore where her parents owned Braganza Hotel (referenced in "Freedom at Midnight" Collins & Lapierre). After studying languages and the arts in Rome and classical piano in London, she moved to Montreal in 1966. Essentially self-taught, her subjects vary from evocative landscapes, lush florals to vibrant figures of Indian women.

She exhibited regularly and established herself as a Quebec artist with a style of her own, using brilliant color and texture to express emotion. Her work is shared with the permission of her beloved son, Miguel, who cared for her the last 13 years of her life. You can see more of her work at www.cherylbraganza.com.

*Cheryl's Story – written by her son, Miguel Da Costa Frias

Some people leave such a ripple on the wave of humanity, that it floats us all toward one another. This was my mother.

A musician with raw unbridled talent, Cheryl was offered a scholarship to Juilliard when she was sixteen. From a young age, she played the piano, the organ, the accordion, and the harmonica with equal versatility. She began to paint in her 20's and discovered that she was a gifted painter.

She was diagnosed with a bone-related cancer on her 60th birthday in 2005 and came a hairsbreadth from death four times, only to fight her way back to life each time. For the last decade, while fighting cancer, a handwritten quote from Goethe rested on top of her easel: "Rest not. Life is sweeping by; go and dare before you die. Something mighty and sublime, leave behind to conquer time." Little did we know how much she would take this quote to heart or put it into action.

Cheryl developed her painting talent with exponential speed. When asked why she was working so feverishly, she answered, "I'm in a race against time. I have so much to say and so much more to bring into the world…" In her last five years of life, she produced more artwork and published more writing than she produced in the previous 20 years.

In 2008, she was named Montreal's Woman of the Year for using her art as a tool to fight for women's rights all over the world. She was featured in hundreds of media worldwide and was then elected President of the prestigious Women's Art Society of Montreal, which she grew dramatically.

Her effect on people became evident in the thousands of emails she received from people she inspired across the world.

She lived longer than anyone in recorded history with myeloma cancer in the brain, and refused painkillers because she didn't want her senses affected. Her only desire was to experience every moment in living color until her very last breath. Following her last remission, limping in pain, she decided to learn jazz from scratch, started her own jazz band and played to sold out crowds in Griffintown for two years.

Our mother believed that in order to enjoy true happiness, she should live each moment as if it were her last. Yesterday will never return. Tomorrow may never happen. While we may speak of the past or of the future, the only reality we have is that of right now, the present instant.

Confronting the reality of death enabled her to blossom with unlimited creativity, courage and joy. The more broken her body became over the years, the more she painted soaring images of birds, and butterflies, and dancing women.

She was never alone, surrounded by an ever-increasing group of family and friends who grew to love her (and each other). When the cancer finally paralyzed her body, it was our turn to bring the joy to her; kidnapping her from the hospital for secret outings, regaling her with live music every day for nine months. And even then, we marveled how she could still paint magical tapestries of colour and love with her face, her voice and her mind.

She died peacefully in her sleep after seeing her three children; her soul soaring to the beautiful places reflected in her art.

Claire Dorey
Goldsmiths: BA Hons Fine Art.
Main Employment: Journalist and Creative, UK and overseas.
Artist: Most notable group show: Pillow Talk at the Tate Modern. Included in the *Pillow Talk* Book.

Curator: 3 x grass roots SLWA exhibitions and educational events on the subject of Female Empowerment, showcasing female artists, academic speeches and local musicians. Silence Is Over – Raising awareness on violence towards women; Ex Voto – Existential Mexican Art Therapy; Heo – Female empowerment in the self-portrait.

Extra study: Suppressed Female History: History of the Goddess; Accessing Creative Wisdom; Sound and Breath Work; Reiki Master; Colour Therapy; Hand Mudras; Reflexology; Sculpture. Teaching Workshops: Sculpture and Drawing.

Deborah A. Meyerriecks is a self-dedicated Witch and Community Priestess. Originally from New York City, she currently lives in the liminal space of the Colorado River Valley in the Mohave Desert of N.W. Arizona. She has offered guidance and spiritual counseling to support others while they discover their own personal right path. Since responding to the Call of The Morrigan and becoming Her priest, her self-healing and shadow work have been exponentially more productive as she navigates her personal lessons this life has to offer. Growing up in the Catholic Church of her mother, Deborah was volun-told into service as a choir member and leader of song, often recreating the lyrics of hymns and singing them on her walk back to the house she grew up in to fit her magick and devotional practices. Deborah's first manuscript, "Macha and the

Medic: Service and Priesthood on the Frontlines of Life" is in editing and an outline for her next book on Shadow-Care has been submitted for consideration. Deborah is currently organizing her first small retreat centered on Shadow-Care, October 2022 in NYS. Contact her at WillowMoon@yahoo.com or www.WillowMoonConsulting.com to see what she's currently offering.

Jeanine Elizabeth Otte (JEO) is a writer, poet, speaker, educator, social change designer-collaborator, advocate, and leader. Jeanine's life mission is to build a world with her community that allows everyone to be fully who they are. Jeanine works and writes at the intersections of nature, race, family, body autonomy, experiences of women and children, and social justice. Jeanine is a certified conversation leader for a caring economy and designs and leads programs that educate and employ people from typically overlooked communities in the fields of renewable energy and sustainability. She is a partner to Carlos, and parent to Malcolm, Michelle, and Nicole. Jeanine is the owner of JEO Speaks LLC and can be found at @jeo_speaks.

Kat Shaw prides herself on breaking through the stereotypical views of beauty that have been cast upon society by the media, having made her name painting the glorious reality that is a woman's body.

Her nude studies of real women garnered unprecedented popularity within only a few short months, as women were crying out for themselves to be portrayed in art, rather than the airbrushed images of the perfection of the female form that are so rife in today's culture.

After graduating with a fine art degree, Kat achieved a successful full-time teaching career for 14 years and continues to teach art part-time whilst passionately pursuing her mission of world domination by empowering as many women as possible to reach their fullest potential by embracing their bodies and loving themselves wholeheartedly.

Kat spreads her inspirational magic through her artwork, her Wellbeing business, "Fabulously Imperfect," and her dedication to Goddess energy.

Reiki is a huge part of her life, and as a Reiki Master, Kat is committed to sharing Reiki, teaching Usui, Angelic and Karuna Reiki, and channelling Reiki energy through her artwork to uplift and heal.

As a Sister of Avalon, Kat also works directly with her Goddess consciousness, connecting to Goddess and Priestess energy and translating it into Divine Feminine infused paintings to inspire women and spread Goddess love.

Kat is also a belly dancer and an avid pioneer to improve the lives of rescue animals, and mum to a gorgeous teenage daughter.

Kate Hilderbrandt is a women's empowerment coach and Co-Creator of Deconstructionaries, a community of women lighting our way out of patriarchy, where she creates courses and leads women's circles. She has also been a poet as long as she can remember. Kate grew up on church music and is proud to participate in giving some of these old hymns new life.

Kay Louise Aldred writes and edits for Girl God Books. She has contributed to the Girl God Anthologies *Warrior Queen, Answering the Call of the Morrigan, In Defiance of Oppression - The Legacy of Boudicca and Just as I am - Hymns Affirming the Divine Female.* Kay will also feature in the Girl God Anthology *Songs of Solstice - Goddess Carols,* scheduled for publication in 2022. Currently she is co-editing the four upcoming Girl God Anthologies: *Re-Membering with Goddess: Healing the Patriarchal Perpetuation of Trauma, The Crone Initiation and Invitation: Women speak on the Menopause Journey, Rainbow*

Goddess - Celebrating Neurodiversity and *Pain Perspectives: Finding Meaning in the Fire*. Scheduled publication for these books is 2022/2023. In addition, Kay is writing her own books. *Mentorship of Goddess: Growing Sacred Womanhood* will be published June 2022 and *Making Love with the Divine: Sacred, Ecstatic, Erotic Experiences* is scheduled for February 2023. Finally, Kay and her husband Dan Aldred, are co-authoring a book together, *Embodied Education*, which will be available September 2023.

Lisbeth Cheever-Gessaman is the artist and illustrator of *The Divine Feminine Oracle* and *The Spellcasting Oracle*. She is a scholar of the Divine Feminine, and a visionary artist who merges magick and technology with traditional mediums to create new interpretations of myth and archetype. Through her work she explores shamanic, astrological and mythological constructs to interpret the liminal worlds of the Divine Feminine, incorporating art and talisman to create a third phenomenon, or magical reality.

In honor of the Great Mother, and as personal witness, she creates all work under the pseudonym "SheWhoIsArt."
Website: www.shewhoisart.com
Facebook: www.facebook.com/shewhoisart
Instagram: shewhois

Liz Childs Kelly is a writer, Sacred Feminine researcher and educator, community builder, initiated priestess in the 13 Moons Lineage, and the host of the *Home to Her* podcast, which is dedicated to amplifying the voices of the Sacred Feminine. She is also the cohost of the Revelry series of online events, which invite women from around the world to participate in ecstatic, embodied celebrations of the gifts of each season, and is in the process of completing her first book, *Home to Her: Reclaiming the Ancient Wisdom of the Sacred Feminine*. She is a mother of two, and currently lives in central Virginia, USA, on the ancestral lands of the Monacan people.

Dr Lynne Sedgmore CBE is a Priestess to Goddess, Poetess, retired Chief Executive, soul coach and Priestess healer. She lives in Glastonbury UK. Her three poetry collections are Enlivenment (Chrysalis Press 2013), Healing through the Goddess (TheaSpeaks Press 2017) and Crone (TheaSpeaks Press 2019). She wrote the Avalon Anthem which opened the famous Glastonbury Festival in 2015. She is founder and tutor of the Goddess Luminary Wheel Leadership trainings, a unique combination of liberating leadership, feminism and Goddess spirituality offered through the Glastonbury Goddess Temple. She has 3 daughters and 2 granddaughters. Her Welsh heritage means she has loved singing hymns since a child.

Michelle Kathleen Elder was raised lukewarm Presbyterian, great-granddaughter of a Welsh minister. As a child, a female relation - who had a beautiful singing voice herself – once admonished her to whisper-sing in church because a woman singing with her full voice would draw too much attention to herself. So Michelle now sings loudly in circles that meet outside under the oaks and cedars; in the car; and occasionally at the local pub on "Beer and Hymns" nights, such as those hosted by the progressive Christian church, Sojourn Grace Collective (*sojourngrace.com*). Michelle blogs at *elderinthewoods.com*.

Monette Chilson has written about the divine feminine for the past decade, authoring *Sophia Rising: Awakening Your Sacred Wisdom Through Yoga* (Bright Sky Press, 2013) and *My Name is Lilith* (Girl God Books, 2017). She co-edited *Original Resistance: Reclaiming Lilith, Reclaiming Ourselves* (Girl God Books, 2019) and wrote the companion *Lilith Circle Guide* for group study in 2021. She has contributed to national magazines, including *Yoga Journal, Integral Yoga Magazine* and *Elephant Journal*. Monette's work has been featured in several anthologies, *Yoga Wisdom: Warrior Tales Inspiring You On and Off Your Mat* and *Whatever Works: Feminists of Faith Speak*. Connect on Twitter, Instagram and Facebook or explore her work at www.MonetteChilson.com.

Pat Daly (editor) is a mother of three daughters and proud grandma. A published author / writer on career and job search issues, Pat lives in Portland, Oregon.

Patricia Lynn Reilly has been inspiring women for over 25 years. Her iconic books, poems, and trainings have traveled around the world. Patricia's books include: *A God Who Looks Like Me: Discovering a Woman-Affirming Spirituality, Be Full of Yourself: The Journey from Self-Criticism to Self-Celebration, Imagine a Woman in Love with Herself: Embracing Your Wholeness & Wisdom, I Promise Myself: Making a Commitment to Yourself & Your Dreams,* and *Words Made Flesh: An Anthology of Poetry and Prose.*

Rebekah Myers is dedicated to opening doors of understanding on behalf of women everywhere. She is the founder/facilitator of Sacred Sisters Full Moon Circle, which serves as a virtual Facebook and Instagram public page, a private Facebook group for women, and an actual women's circle that meets in-person. For International Women's Day in March of 2018, Rebekah was honored to have been one of five women recognized by KSL as Utah's most inspirational women.

Through her social anthropologist parents, Rebekah spent memorable time with the Iroquois (a matrilineal people) of Six Nations Reserve in Ontario, Canada. This experience significantly informed her life for the good. Rebekah has had a life-long interest in and passion for folklore, mythology, and ancient history, and has spent significant time in these worlds. Although Rebekah formally came later in life to women's spirituality, she has found such fulfillment on this path, that there is no turning back. As a writer, teacher, director, award-winning singer/performer/actress, mother, grandmother, and wedding officiator, Rebekah works to empower, enlighten, and uplift women and their brothers. She knows it is possible to heal the wounds of patriarchy and live with depth, meaning, and joy.

Ruth Calder-Murphy is a creative artist, teacher, wife and mother living in London, UK. She is passionate about celebrating the uniqueness and diversity of people, questioning the unquestionable and discovering new perspectives on old wonders. She is learning to ride the waves that come along – peaks and troughs – and how to cling on to whatever's available when the waves become too stormy to ride. You can visit Ruth on her website at arciemme.com or on her Facebook page: Paradoxologies.

Sharon Smith is a writer, ghost writer, editor, and proofreader with a passion for helping women reconnect with their Authentic Selves and Voices. She loves and honors the Great Mother in all Her many forms, and has a deep connection to Nature. She identifies as a Green Witch and follows an eclectic spiritual path that is a blending of Native American and Celtic Teachings, both in her ancestral line.

Painting is **Sue Ellen Parkinson's** doorway through to understanding the world. Creativity is her form of prayer. When she paints a person, she is honoring that Being. That experience is one of deep connection that brings her into wholeness. That's as important to her as oxygen. Her focus is largely about re-visioning, and celebrating womankind—lifting them up. Exploring the Christian mystics has produced a profound change in her. She has found herself particularly drawn to Mary Magdalene. For her, Magdalene is the archetype who represents All Women who have been inaccurately portrayed in history. It's been a healing experience to restore her identity, and the identity of other great women, to the wise and sovereign beings that she believes they are. In so doing, she has become more empowered herself. www.sueellenparkinson.com

Susan Klahr was an important force within the intellectual and artistic community that makes El Paso/Juárez unique along the U.S./Mexico Border and in the United States. Her art spoke of the world she witnessed before her, especially the people that populated her imagination, people who in Susan's paintings radiate a spiritual presence. She is quoted as saying, "I'm part of the story, it's my story now and it goes on and on and on."

Susan died New Year's morning 2010. She had been struggling with cancer for several years, and finally the disease asked her to cross to the other side. She is survived by her husband David and her two sons Sito and Arlo. Her work is shared with the permission of her family. (Bio adapted from Cinco Puntos Press.)

Trista Hendren founded Girl God Books in 2011 to support a necessary unraveling of the patriarchal world view of divinity. Her first book—*The Girl God*, a children's picture book—was a response to her own daughter's inability to see herself reflected in God. Since then, she has published more than 40 books by a dozen women from across the globe with help from her family and friends. Originally from Portland, Oregon, she lives in Bergen, Norway. You can learn more about her projects at www.thegirlgod.com.

Trista's Acknowledgments

I would like to acknowledge my co-editors. My mother, **Pat Daly,** has edited each and every one of my books. There would be no Girl God Books without her many contributions. I was thrilled to also work with my dear Sister **Sharon Smith** on this project—who shares my passion for dismantling all things patriarchal. Special thanks to Sharon for singing through each hymn and pouring through the meaning of each and every word in this book.

Appreciation to my beloved husband **Anders Løberg**, who designed the book cover and helped with website updates. Your love, support and many contributions made this book possible.

Tremendous gratitude to the fabulous **Kat Shaw** for allowing us to feature her gorgeous painting as the cover art.

Special thanks to **Deborah Meyerriecks** for stepping in to help me with several hymns I was stuck on. These were on my must-have list—so I greatly appreciate her time and talent in re-writing them.

I would also like to acknowledge **Shellee Layne** for her work on bringing these Herms to life on Instagram Live and our Zoom Sing-Alongs. Her rendition of *How Great the Mothers Love for Us* was especially healing for me.

My mom and I would also like to acknowledge her wonderful partner, **Rick Weiss,** for being an all-around awesome guy—and helping us with the page numbers.

Lastly, I would like to thank my dear sisters **Tamara Albanna, Alyscia Cunningham, Susan Morgaine, Jeanette Bjørnsen, Camilla Berge Wolff, Tammy Nedrebø-Skurtveit, Sharon Smith, Arlene Bailey** and **Kay Louise Aldred** and for always being right there to cheer me on in the spirit of true sisterhood.

Thank you to all our readers and Girl God supporters over the years. We love and appreciate you!

Sharon's Acknowledgments

I would like to acknowledge, first and foremost, my Dear Sister **Trista Hendren** for giving me the opportunity to be a part of Girl God Books. When I first discovered the Girl God FB page, I knew I was "home." And when Trista messaged me one day and asked if I would like to write something for her anthology, *On the Wings of Isis: Reclaiming the Sovereignty of Auset*, I was deeply touched and incredibly honored. Since then I have had several poems, articles and even a bit of my own original artwork in various other Girl God Books anthologies. Trista, you made my dream of becoming a published author a reality, and I can never thank you enough for that!

I want to thank **Pat Daly**, as well, for her dedication with helping to edit/proof this book and all of the Girl God Books publications. It is no easy job to be an editor/proofreader (I have done this professionally for many years, so I know)—her work here is deeply appreciated!

I would also like to thank my daughter, **Kelinda**, my greatest cheerleader, who believed in my ability to be a published writer, even when I didn't. I Love You, my Flame-haired Warrior Woman! Three hand squeezes!

Thanks also to my long-time sister-friend, **Dr. Bambi Lobdell, Ph.D.,** professor of English and Women's Studies at both the University of Binghamton and SUNY Oneonta in upstate New York, who created the course of study, "Witches, Whores, and Wild Women" and who authored the incredible book, *A Strange Sort of Being: The Transgender Life of Lucy Ann/Joseph Israel Lobdell, 1829-1912*, about one of her role-breaking ancestors. Bambi has been my inspiration since our days together at The Delaware River Writers Group, and she continues to inspire me to accomplish my goals as a writer, a story-teller, and a teacher.

Much gratitude to my mentor and dear sister-friend, **Colleen Russell, M.A.** Transpersonal Psychology, a student of Marion Woodman, an artist/writer (The Feminine Path to Wholeness: Becoming a Conscious Queen) and co-facilitator of women's retreats at beautiful Scotia House in the Pacific Northwest. Colleen guided me on my Healing Journey as a woman seeking to reconnect with her authentic self and voice. Colleen's wisdom and gentle teachings changed my life!

Thanks, as well, to my dear sister (and the Scotia House Fairy), **Sandee Meade**, whose constant support and encouragement enabled me to begin to believe in myself. Thanks for allowing me to live at Scotia House and heal there for two years: It was MAGICAL!

And finally, thanks and so much love to the following young women whom I've heart-adopted over the years, who have blessed my life in so many ways: **Angie Metzner**, **Michele Chaney**, **Karen Pogorzelski**, and **Renee Jamerson**. You are each amazing young women — Overcomers and Wise, Wild Women in your own right. I am so immensely proud of you all and so honored to consider you "heart-daughters"!

If you enjoyed this book, please consider writing a brief review on Amazon and/or Goodreads.

Songs of Solstice: Goddess Carols – Edited by Trista Hendren, Sharon Smith and Pat Daly

Goddess Chants and Songs Book – Edited by Trista Hendren, Anique Radiant Heart and Pat Daly

Re-Membering with Goddess: Healing the Patriarchal Perpetuation of Trauma – Edited by Kay Louise Aldred, Trista Hendren and Pat Daly

Mentorship with Goddess: Growing Sacred Womanhood – Written by Kay Louise Aldred

Lotus Heart: The Compassion of Kuan Yin – Edited by Trista Hendren, Herng Yu Tzong, and Yeshe Matthews

And Still, I Rise – Kat Shaw

The Crone Initiation: Women Speak on the Menopause Journey – Edited by Kay Louise Aldred, Trista Hendren and Pat Daly

Rainbow Goddess - Celebrating Neurodiversity – Edited by Kay Louise Aldred, Trista Hendren and Tamara Albanna

Pain Perspectives: Finding Meaning in the Fire – Edited by Kay Louise Aldred, Trista Hendren and Pat Daly

Embodied Education – Kay Louise Aldred and Dan Aldred

My Name is Brigid – Written by Isca Johnson and Illustrated by Barbara O'Meara

http://thegirlgod.com/publishing.php

9 788829 372521